NEW DIRECTIONS FOR STUDENT SERVI

John H. Schuh, *Iowa State University*
EDITOR-IN-CHIEF

Elizabeth J. Whitt, *University of Iowa*
ASSOCIATE EDITOR

Understanding and Applying Cognitive Development Theory

Patrick G. Love
Kent State University

Victoria L. Guthrie
Ohio University

AUTHORS

Number 88, Winter 1999

JOSSEY-BASS PUBLISHERS
San Francisco

UNDERSTANDING AND APPLYING COGNITIVE DEVELOPMENT THEORY
Patrick G. Love, Victoria L. Guthrie (aus.)
New Directions for Student Services, no. 88
John H. Schuh, Editor-in-Chief
Elizabeth J. Whitt, Associate Editor

ISSN 0164-7970   ISBN 0-7879-4870-5

NEW DIRECTIONS FOR STUDENT SERVICES is part of The Jossey-Bass Higher and Adult Education Series and is published quarterly by Jossey-Bass Inc., Publishers, 350 Sansome Street, San Francisco, California 94104-1342. Periodicals postage paid at San Francisco, California, and at additional mailing offices. Postmaster: Send address changes to New Directions for Student Services, Jossey-Bass Inc., Publishers, 350 Sansome Street, San Francisco, California 94104-1342.

New Directions for Student Services is indexed in College Student Personnel Abstracts and Contents Pages in Education.

SUBSCRIPTIONS cost $58.00 for individuals and $104.00 for institutions, agencies, and libraries. See ordering information page at end of book.

EDITORIAL CORRESPONDENCE should be sent to the Editor-in-Chief, John H. Schuh, N 243 Lagomarcino Hall, Iowa State University, Ames, Iowa 50011

Cover photograph by Wernher Krutein/PHOTOVAULT © 1990.

Jossey-Bass Web address: www.josseybass.com

CONTENTS

Authors' Notes

At the heart of student affairs work should be a focus on student learning (American College Personnel Association, 1994; Wingspread Group on Higher Education, 1993). Indeed, the *Principles of Good Practice for Student Affairs,* jointly authored by the American College Personnel Association and the National Association of Student Personnel Administrators (1997), stresses the creation of learning environments and learning experiences for students as a primary purpose underlying good practice in our field. "The Student Learning Imperative" (Schroeder, 1996, p. 119) also underscores that "student affairs professionals are educators who share responsibility with faculty, academic administrators, other staff and students themselves for creating the conditions under which students are likely to expend time and energy in educationally-purposeful activities." Creating conditions that inspire students to devote time and energy to these educationally purposeful activities, both in and outside the classroom, is key to enhancing student learning and personal development (American College Personnel Association, 1994). One of the hallmarks of a learned and developed person is complex cognitive skills. Fortunately, student affairs educators have a broad base of theory and research on which to base intentional interventions and activities directed toward enhancing the cognitive development of college students.

Cognitive development has been a focus of social sciences research for much of the twentieth century. Two streams of research developed early in this century. One stream focused on the concept of intelligence and quickly captured the public's attention with tests purporting to measure one's intellectual potential, or "intelligence quotient" (IQ). Although the notion of IQ has come under scrutiny during the last several decades, tributaries of this stream can still be seen today. Standardized aptitude tests are direct descendants of intelligence testing. Howard Gardner's work (1993) in identifying, describing, and creating curricula for multiple intelligences is another example of important work in the general area of intelligence.

The other stream of research on the human faculties focused on the process of cognition and the development of cognitive abilities. Jean Piaget's work (1969; Piaget and Inhelder, 1971) in the development of formal reasoning in children is perhaps the most well known of this genre. Another important figure was Lev Vygotsky (1978), whose work in the areas now known as social cognition and constructivism was conducted in the 1920s and 1930s in Soviet

We wish to thank Patricia King for her assistance; Marianne T. Bock and Dianne Runnestrand for their ideas, suggestions, editing, and gentle critique; and Nadine Hagoort, Vicki Hellman, and the other students in college student development courses at Kent State University and Ohio University who contributed insights and provided feedback on the manuscript.

Russia but only became known in the West during the last twenty-five years. After World War II, research relating to cognition expanded to include such topics as information processing, metacognition, and learning theory.

The focus of this volume is on the cognitive development of college students. Virtually all cognitive development theories of student development trace their origins to Piaget's work. The five theories reviewed in this volume are no exception. They seek to describe the process of change in cognitive structures students use in making meaning of their world, with a focus on *how* meaning is structured, not on *what* is known or believed.

William Perry (1970) was the first researcher to focus solely on the cognitive development of college students, and his work grew directly from Piaget's. Perry conducted his research in the 1950s and 1960s, and it was first published in 1968. In 1978, *Applying New Developmental Findings* (Knefelkamp, Widick, and Parker) summarized the major college student development theories of that time; Perry's intellectual development scheme was among them. Since the publication of that popular and timely volume, the research on college student development has grown tremendously, and student development models and theories have proliferated. A concise summary of all major theories in a monograph-sized volume is no longer possible. However, a summary of college student cognitive development theory is an attainable goal. The theories that are the focus of this volume are those of Perry (1970), Belenky, Clinchy, Goldberger, and Tarule (1986), King and Kitchener (1994), Baxter Magolda (1992), and Kegan (1982, 1994). These theories vary in a number of important ways, including the structure of the developmental process; the endpoints; and the number, characteristics, and labeling of stages or dimensions. At the same time, there are commonalities in substance and process among the theories, which we address in the final chapter.

The focus of this monograph is on understanding and applying cognitive development theory. Therefore, it concentrates on explaining the various theories and translating them into practice in student affairs. As Piper and Rodgers (1992) point out, in order to apply a theory of student development, one must first know that theory in depth. The summaries in this monograph provide a starting point for reaching an in-depth understanding of these vital theories. We recommend that readers explore the original sources for a deeper and more thorough understanding.

We intend this volume for student affairs practitioners who want a grounding in cognitive development theory. We also hope that graduate faculty and students in graduate preparation programs will find the volume useful in developing an understanding of this important area of student development theory; from that understanding, competence in intentional informal assessment and application of theory in practice may grow.

A number of other researchers have expanded on and extended the theoretical foundation of cognitive development of college students that was laid by William Perry's groundbreaking research (which is summarized in

Chapter One). *Women's Ways of Knowing* (Belenky, Clinchy, Goldberger, and Tarule, 1986), though not argued by its authors to be a formal theory, is the report of research on cognitive development and the making of meaning as experienced by women. Belenky, Clinchy, Goldberger, and Tarule, whose research is the topic of Chapter Two, extend Perry's work to women and also to women of lower socioeconomic status (Perry studied affluent Harvard students of the 1950s and 1960s). Marcia Baxter Magolda's epistemological reflection model (addressed in Chapter Three) grew out of her dissertation research on Perry's scheme, as did Patricia King and Karen Kitchener's reflective judgment model (reviewed in Chapter Four). Both of these models have become important elements of the discourse in student affairs related to student development in general and to cognitive development and learning in particular.

Chapters One through Four of this volume begin with an overview of the theory and the research on which the theory is based. This is followed by an explication of the theory and an exploration of some of the applications for student affairs practice (except for Chapter One, which instead addresses the saliency of the theory for today's student affairs professionals).

The influence of varying social contexts and emotional states on the cognitive development of students has become a focus of consideration in general and in the field of student affairs in particular (Goleman, 1995; Love and Goodsell Love, 1995; Lundeberg and Diemert Moch, 1995). Chapter Five centers on this research area. Robert Kegan's theory of meaning formation (1982, 1994), somewhat influenced by Perry's research, also incorporates social, cultural, and emotional processes. Chapter Six considers Kegan's orders of consciousness. Chapter Seven synthesizes the research described in this volume, introduces a model of intentional informal assessment of the cognitive development of students to be used in student affairs practice, and explores ways these theories can be applied in our work.

Patrick G. Love
Victoria L. Guthrie
Authors

PATRICK G. LOVE is associate professor and coordinator of the master's degree program in higher education and student personnel at Kent State University.

VICTORIA L. GUTHRIE is assistant professor of higher education and student personnel leadership at Ohio University.

1

William Perry's intellectual scheme set the stage for future theory building related to the cognitive development of college students.

Perry's Intellectual Scheme

Little can be said about Perry's scheme of intellectual and ethical development that has not been said already; however, any discussion of cognitive development theories of college students must begin with William Perry's work. Among the reasons for including Perry are that three of the works also summarized in this volume (Baxter Magolda, 1992; Belenky, Clinchy, Goldberger, and Tarule, 1986; King and Kitchener, 1994) grew out of the research of Perry and his colleagues. In addition, the theory—and what it has to say about the cognitive development of college students—is still salient for today's practitioners. At a minimum Perry's work has intuitive face validity for practitioners (King, 1978), and it forms a bridge from the child and adolescent studies of Piaget, Vygotsky, and others to a more direct focus on early adulthood, especially the early adulthood of college students.

Two of the most cited and thorough reviews of Perry's theory and research are King's chapter (1978) and Perry's own synopsis (1981). Briefer, but more recent, reviews include Chickering and Reisser's summary (1993) in *Education and Identity* and Evans, Forney, and Guido-DiBrito's summary (1998) in *Student Development in College*. The purpose of this chapter is to provide a summary of Perry's work and view it in the context of the late 1990s. Perry was a counselor and professor of education at Harvard, and during the course of about fifteen years in the 1950s and 1960s he worked with more than thirty people in conducting the research that led to the development of this scheme (Perry, 1981). Perry and his colleagues came up with the intellectual and ethical scheme now identified solely with him. One of his motives for studying the cognitive development of college students was his recognition of the increasing relativism in society and diversity on campus,

---

For ease of communication, throughout this volume we refer to the scheme as Perry's, as has been the tradition.

which had both been accelerating since World War II. Perry felt that there was a need to comprehend how students came to understand the modern world through multiple frames of reference. The diversity Perry identified was geographic diversity—students were arriving at Harvard and Radcliffe from all over the United States and from throughout the world. This kind of diversity is distantly related to today's concerns about such issues as class, race or ethnicity, and sexual orientation.

The population Perry and his colleagues studied consisted of white, overwhelmingly male, upper-class students at Harvard and Radcliffe—the elite of the time. They interviewed students at the end of each academic year during their four years in college. Each interview began with the same question: "What stands out for you from the past year?" They interviewed 31 students from the class of 1958 (27 from Harvard, 4 from Radcliffe), and then 109 students from the classes of 1962 and 1963 (85 from Harvard, 24 from Radcliffe). A total of 464 interviews were conducted from which there were complete four-year sequences for 84 students, of which only 2 were women. Their conclusion was that, although the content of the interviews varied tremendously, the underlying structures of meaning making (that is, the forms students used to make sense of their academic and personal experiences) and the sequence of development were equivalent. Also, they concluded that the differences were not due solely to personality styles but to different aspects of a developmental process.

Perry's work was an outgrowth of theories that preceded his own, especially Piaget's theory. For example, Perry and his colleagues adopted Piaget's terms *assimilation* and *accommodation* to describe the processes of development they discovered in the students they interviewed. Perry (1970, p. 204) also pointed out the similarity between the two theories as a "movement away from a naive egocentrism to a differentiated awareness of the environment." Both theories trace a process of new awareness of the self, of environmental influences on the self, and of the complex balance between this emerging awareness of the self and the external influences from the environment. Perry's focus on college students extends our understanding of cognitive development beyond Piaget, whose theory stopped at approximately age fifteen.

Terms and Concepts

In some cases, Perry and his colleagues developed a specific vocabulary to explain what they were finding in their research. Definitions of some of the important terms and concepts that will be elucidated in the course of this chapter are presented here.

Position. Perry's scheme comprises nine positions. He chose to use the term *position* rather than *stage*. *Stage* refers to a relatively stable and enduring form, pattern, or structure of meaning making that pervades a person's experience (Perry, 1970). Perry and his colleagues preferred the term *posi-*

tion because they made no assumptions about the duration of the position. Amid the variety and range of structures a particular student uses to make sense of the various aspects of the world at any particular point in time, *position* could express a central tendency in students' meaning making. Also, the term implies the "place," or vantage point, from which the student views the world (Perry, 1970).

Absolute.   Perry used the term *Absolute* (uppercase A) synonymously with Truth—in the sense of unchanging, universal, timeless facts and knowledge. The Truth was possessed by Authorities.

Authorities.   *Authorities* (uppercase A) were the possessors of the right answers in the Absolute; *authorities* (lowercase a) existed in the relativistic world and derived their authority from many sources, such as power, expertise, training, wisdom, experience, and position.

Adherence and Opposition.   In several of the early positions of the scheme, Perry and his colleagues noticed that students differed in their perceived relationship with Authorities. Those identified as *adherents* tended to identify and align with Authorities through a dualistic structure of the world: Authorities were part of "we" (Authority-we-right). Those identified as being in *opposition* set themselves apart from Authorities: Authorities were part of "they," and they were wrong (Authority-they-wrong; we-right). These different relationships with and to Authority had an influence on the form of students' intellectual development.

Alternatives to Growth.   In his original work, Perry (1970) identified at least three alternatives to forward progress through the positions of his scheme: *temporizing, retreat,* and *escape.* Knefelkamp (1999) identified at least one more: *functional regression.*

Temporizing occurred when a student delayed in one position for a period of time, hesitating to take the next step. The individual usually was aware of the position ahead but was unwilling to proceed.

Retreat described a movement back to the relative safety and security of dualism—a world where right and wrong were clear and ambiguity did not exist. This occurred often in reaction to the complicated nature of pluralism.

Escape described the act students engaged in when they avoided moving beyond the position of relativism to the responsibility of making commitments in a relativistic world. Students who took the escape route realized that it was easier to remain in a relativistic stance than to face the difficulty of making commitments and personal choices.

Functional regression described a process where students who were undertaking new learning in a new environment "functionally" regressed to previous positions until they felt comfortable in the new environment. That is, the regression was developmentally appropriate; to progress developmentally, the students needed to move back to previous sense making in order to get their bearings.

Perry's Nine Positions of Cognitive Development

Perry's scheme has been divided and sorted in a variety of ways. In various explications, it has been broken down into nine, four, three, or two parts. As already indicated, his theory lists nine separate positions. However, they often are clustered into groups for easier digestion and initial understanding. Several authors (such as Brand, 1988; King, 1978; and Kloss, 1994) suggest that the dominant pattern is four major groups within the nine positions: dualism (positions 1 and 2), multiplicity (positions 3 and 4a), relativism (positions 4b, 5, and 6), and commitment in relativism (positions 7, 8, and 9). Perry (1970) himself initially clustered them into three groups. He described positions 1, 2, and 3 as the transition from a right-wrong outlook to the recognition of relativism; positions 4, 5, and 6 as the development of this relativistic outlook; and positions 7, 8, and 9 as the development of commitments in a relativistic world. However, the scheme also can be seen as having two major orientations: pre–position 5 (knowledge and values are objective, certain, and universal); position 5 and post–position 5 (knowledge and values are relative, contingent, and contextual). Position 5 is where the most significant revolution in sense making occurs for the individual (Perry, 1970). It is this dichotomy that led to King's criticism (1978) of Perry's theory, in which King contends that the first five positions described epistemological and intellectual development and that the last four described moral, ethical, and identity development. This chapter focuses on the first five positions of Perry's scheme and the transitions between them. (The last four positions of Perry's scheme were lightly drawn and in the intervening years have not been filled in. Instead, ethical and moral development has arisen as a separate area of focus and research.) Providing information on the transitions between positions allows for clearer application of the theory in practice (Perry, 1981). To further enhance clarity, Knefelkamp's labels (1999), which she indicated she and Perry developed to clarify confusion about the original labels, are given in parentheses, either following the subheading of the section where the label is discussed (for positions 1–5) or within the text of that section (for positions 6–9). For example, Knefelkamp's label for basic dualism is *strict dualism*.

Position 1: Basic Dualism (Strict Dualism). For those who view their experience from this position, the world is divided into absolutes (right and wrong, good and bad). Everything is known. Authorities possess the Absolute Truth; they know the right answers and identify what is good (Perry, 1970). The world of Authority is free from conflict, and a student's job is to listen to the Authorities in order to receive the right answers—the Truth. All problems are solvable by obeying and conforming to what is right and what Authorities want.

Perry and his colleagues did not find any students who by the end of their first year in college had basic dualism as a dominant orientation (Perry, 1970). However, the expectation associated with dualism (the existence of right answers for all questions and problems) persists as an important assumption underlying the first four positions of the scheme. It is only in position 5 that the discovery of a simple right answer becomes recognized as the exception rather than as the rule.

Transition to Position 2. Development is prompted by the recognition of the existence of different opinions and the recognition that some Authorities disagree on what is right and good (Perry, 1981). In Perry's original work (1970), he noted that students were confronted with pluralism and diversity of opinions most powerfully in the residence halls and that the first challenge to basic dualism often came from peers.

Position 2: Multiplicity Prelegitimate (Strict Dualism). *Multiplicity* refers to the pluralism of answers, opinions, ideas, and points of view related to problems and issues. The notion of multiplicity being "prelegitimate" means that students recognize but stand in opposition to pluralism, complexity, diversity, abstractness, and interpretation. In this position the student remains loyal to Authority, still seeking truth from professionals, such as a professor or advisor, or from books written by "experts." Perry (1970) noted that students at this position also express fear, stress, and sadness when they realize that the way they have known (that is, the world as absolutely known and knowable) is at times no longer in evidence. Because multiplicity is not perceived as legitimate, students must make sense of its existence. They will, for example, allow a difference of opinion but recognize it as only temporary or decide that questions without clear-cut answers are used by Authorities for the purpose of making students think more. Students at this position will also differentiate between good Authorities ("My professor wrote the book on this subject.") and bad Authorities ("She's only a teacher's assistant. What would she know?").

Transition to Position 3. Progression toward the outlook that pluralism may be a legitimate notion is prompted when students experience good Authorities admitting that even they do not have all the answers yet (Perry, 1981). Students struggling with this transition may divide subjects into the definite (most often math and science) and the vague (such as social sciences and humanities) (Perry, 1981).

Position 3: Multiplicity Legitimate but Subordinate (Early Multiplicity). Students who view the world from this position accept as legitimate the idea that there is room for human uncertainty but that this uncertainty does not affect the nature of Truth itself because the uncertainty is temporary (Perry, 1970). The limit of uncertainty that students can tolerate has expanded, but uncertainty is still agitating. Eventually, the one right and universal answer will be found. However, where there is no agreement as to the right and good answer, there is then no wrong answer. Instead, in areas of uncertainty everyone is viewed as having a right to a personal opinion. Rightness, therefore, vanishes as a standard of evaluation. For example, students who see the world from this position begin to question systems of grading or modes of evaluation (in and out of the classroom). If there are no agreed-on answers, nothing is left for a basis of the judgment of schoolwork but style and good expression. Students set out on a quest to discover what the Authorities (that is, professors) want and then try to give it to them (Perry, 1970).

Transition to Position 4. Students recognize that uncertainty is not isolated but widespread and that the chance of quick answers coming soon is slim. Uncertainty is now unavoidable, and the strong identification of Authorities with Absolute truth is further loosened (Perry, 1981).

Position 4: Late Multiplicity. In Perry's original work (1970), position 4 represented the modal starting point of freshmen at the end of their first year. In the earlier positions of the scheme, Perry (1970) described how students varied in how they experienced and worked through their development. However, in position 4 the differences were so dichotomized that Perry and his colleagues identified two different paths students took. Basically, students split into two groups in position 4, only to be reunited in position 5. In 1981, Perry noted that some students may actually proceed from 4a to 4b before moving on to position 5. Perry and his colleagues also found that the path students took seemed to be dictated by their relationship and identification with Authority—that is, the balance between a student's tendency toward Opposition on the one hand and Adherence on the other.

Position 4a: Multiplicity Correlate (Oppositional Alternative). Perry's description (1981, p. 84) of students' mind-set in position 4a was as follows: "These students create the double dualism of a world in which the Authority's right-wrong world is one element and personalistic diversity [multiplicity] is the other. The students have thus succeeded in preserving a dualistic structure for their worlds and at the same time have carved out for themselves a domain promising absolute freedom. In saying in this domain, 'Everyone has a right to [their] own opinion,' students are also saying, 'Where Authorities do not know the Answer, any opinion is as good as any other.'"

Perry's double dualism involved seeing all issues in the world falling into two categories. For many issues and questions, Authorities had the right answers. In this category the student viewed the world dualistically. Regarding issues and questions for which there were no clear-cut answers, the student felt that everyone had a right to a personal opinion. As long as ambiguity remains, people have a right to their own opinion, and no one has the right to call anyone wrong. In this position students claim multiplicity as a domain of their own, equal in legitimacy—a correlate—to Authority's domain (that is, where Truth is known) (Perry, 1970). Perry (1981) argued that multiplicity should not be dismissed as mere license to discount others who disagree with one's opinions. Instead, he pointed out, the egalitarian spirit (the belief that all opinions have equal worth and validity) "expresses a respect for others through a respect for their views" (p. 85).

Transition to Position 4b. In arguing with Authorities (such as teachers), students can become trapped by their own argumentativeness. "Unable to leave well enough alone, [students] demand that Authority justify itself by *reasons* and . . . by *evidence*" in order to prove this or that opinion any more worthwhile than their own (Perry, 1970, p. 99). Unwittingly, students then are caught in the necessity of justifying their opinions and judgments as well, which is a hallmark of relativistic sense making. "The establishment of a domain separate and equal to that of Authority, in which the self takes a stand in chaos, will provide (once contextual thought is discovered to provide some order) a platform from which Authority may be viewed with entirely new eyes. . . . The bridge to the new world is the distinction between an opinion and a supported opinion" (Perry, 1970, pp. 99–100).

Position 4b: Relativism Subordinate (Adherence Alternative). Someone viewing the world from a multiplistic position recognizes diversity, ambiguity, and differences of opinion. A view of the world from a relativistic position does as well, but this position goes beyond multiplicity in that issues of context and rules of evidence are incorporated in order to allow for analysis, comparison, and evaluation of opinions, points of view, and interpretations (Perry, 1970). Knowledge is viewed as contingent and contextual; ideas are better or worse rather than right or wrong. Students who make sense of the world from position 4b recognize these aspects of relativism but still see relativism as subordinate to the overall multiplistic nature of the world.

Perry and his colleagues determined that the majority of college students they studied followed this path through position 4. The shift in this position is from "what they want" (position 3) to "the way they want us to think." For example, in certain courses instructors are not expecting a right answer but are looking for students to provide supporting evidence and arguments for their answers. The paradox that Perry (1970) discovered was that these students were trying to learn to think independently and critically out of a desire to conform to the expectations of Authorities. In this position "'reasoning' provides the lever that will move knowledge from the dualistic realm to the qualitative. . . . The requirement that an answer or opinion be reason*able* raises the possibility that some questions may have *some* legitimate answers" and that some answers will be more legitimate than others (Perry, 1970, p. 102).

Transition to Position 5. As students become more aware of the wide influence of context and rules of evidence, they move from seeing relativistic thought as a special case to recognizing that relativistic thinking will be required more frequently and will work more frequently both in coursework and outside of academics.

Position 5: Relativism (Contextual Relativism, Relational Knowing). As Perry (1970, p. 109) observed, "Up to this point students have been able to assimilate [new ways of thinking] to the fundamentally dualistic structure with which they began." Accommodation has resulted either in a double dualism (position 4a) or the adding of a subcategory of "critical thinking" (position 4b) (Perry, 1970). Movement to position 5, however, involves adopting a way of understanding, analyzing, and evaluating that requires a radical reperception of all knowledge and values as contextual and relativistic. The actions required of position 5 thinking also encourage the development and practice of metacognition—the capacity to think about and examine one's own thinking. Perry (1981) noted that ten years after he first articulated his scheme of development, the modal position for students at the end of their first year at Harvard and Radcliffe had moved from position 4 to position 5.

In the movement to position 5, relativistic thinking becomes normalized and habitual; it is first conscious, then automatic (Perry, 1970). Complexity is expected, and the simplicity of dualism is consigned to the subordinate status of a special case. The notion of Authority becomes *authority*, that is, authority loses its status as not being open to challenge. Instead, authority's assertions are now open to analysis, evaluation, and the requirements of contextualized evidence. Students recognize the existence of multiple (and often conflicting) authorities. Authorities are recognized as groping in a relativistic world along with the students, though they may be more advanced in their experience and in their expertise in groping (Perry, 1970).

Perry (1970) pointed out that this revolution in the way of making sense of the world is both the most violent accommodation of structure and the most quiet. Whereas students were conscious of and remembered the assimilations they had made within and between other positions, they often did not remember their accommodation to position 5 sense making. Students commonly found themselves in a relativistic world without an explicit memory of how they arrived. The salient qualities of this position are a breakdown of the old structure and identity, balanced by a realization of growth and competence in a relativistic world; a changed relationship to authority; a new capacity for detachment; and an awareness of a path toward a new identity through personal commitment (Perry, 1970). To observe both an act and its context one must have an alternate context in which to stand. Relativism provides the ground for detachment and objectivity. In their records (Perry, 1970) no student who had once accepted a relativistic epistemology showed evidence of a generalized regression to absolutism.

Positions 6–9: Commitment in Relativism. Perry (1970) argued that in relativism one is threatened with unbearable disorientation and that students had three alternatives: to go limp, become an active opportunist, or transcend the disorientation through commitment. In position 6 (commitment foreseen) students see that commitments will need to be made in order to establish their bearings in a relativistic world. At this point students feel the beginnings of a desire to define their personal choices, believing that to remain undefined or uncommitted would be irresponsible. Yet those in position 6 still are unable to make a decision, establish a commitment, or narrow their range of possibilities. Positions 7–9 (initial commitment, orientation in implications in commitment, and developing commitments) attempt to chart the diffusion of commitments throughout one's life. As indicated earlier, these positions were not developed adequately in the initial publication of the scheme; in fact, the last three were collapsed into one chapter in the original work (Perry, 1970). In a subsequent explication of the theory (Perry, 1981), positions 7–9 (evolving commitments) consumed less than two pages of a forty-page chapter.

There is at least one major concern with the latter part of Perry's scheme. Although one cannot deny that making commitments is an important aspect of adult life, making commitments and enacting values are part of one's entire life. Establishing priorities and making choices are aspects of the entire life span. The structure of Perry's scheme implies that commitments are made only when one reaches the level of contextual sense making—that where intellectual development ends, ethical development begins (King, 1978). Researchers and theorists who followed Perry do not incorporate this element into their schemes of intellectual development. Likewise, Fowler's theory of faith development (1981), which is based on Perry's work, recognizes the role of values throughout the course of development.

Saliency and Use of Perry's Theory Today

Perry's scheme still has saliency today because the basic underlying structure—movement from a right-wrong mentality, to one in which multiple viewpoints are experienced as valid, and finally to one in which evaluations of evidence are made in a relativistic world—remains viable. Kurfiss (1975, 1977) validated the sequence and cohesiveness of Perry's positions using a sample of sophomores and juniors at a large state university. Although both King and Kitchener's research (1994) and Baxter Magolda's (1992) research differ, and at points diverge, from Perry's in important ways (see Chapters Three and Four), they also bear out Perry's pattern of development.

Other issues need to be considered when interpreting Perry's research for use today. These issues include comparing the sociohistorical context of the time Perry conducted his research with today's context and understanding the changes in college students during the past forty years.

Sociohistorical Context. In trying to use Perry's work for today's professionals and today's students, one needs to consider the sociohistorical context of the 1950s and early 1960s. The latter years of the 1960s were turbulent and witnessed a dramatic reduction in the respect afforded authorities across the societal spectrum. Influences included the Vietnam War and the antiwar protests it generated; the Civil Rights movement; the assassinations of John F. Kennedy, Martin Luther King Jr., and Robert F. Kennedy; rebellion on campuses; the final dismantling of in loco parentis; and the proliferation of coed residence halls and coed universities. The questioning of religious and political leaders and challenges to social scientific dogma accelerated throughout the 1960s as well. All of this might suggest why more students in the 1960s were arriving at Harvard a full position ahead of their counterparts from the 1950s (Perry, 1981). Perhaps they were already practiced at questioning authority and had already struggled with making sense of the multiple, conflicting messages coming at them from their parents, the media, religious organizations, and educators.

Changes in College Students. Perry noted in 1981 that the cohort of students he and his colleagues followed in the 1970s had already experienced the radical transformation that occurs as one reaches position 5. However, other researchers during that same time period (such as Blake, 1976; Meyer, 1977) found a much different developmental picture at institutions less elite than Harvard and Radcliffe. Students at other institutions appeared to enter college at positions 2 or 3 and *graduate* at positions 3 to 5. Therefore, some students managed to graduate from college without having made the significant shift to position 5 thinking. This coincides with Pascarella and Terenzini's (1991) finding that from an individual psychosocial perspective (specifically related to issues of self and identity) many students graduate from college developmentally untouched by the experience.

In looking at today's college student one must also recognize just how different the population of students today is from the students of Harvard in the 1950s. First, there is the oft cited issue of the homogeneity of Perry's participants—traditional-aged, male, upper-middle-class, white. Additionally, it can be assumed that these students also were single, attending full-time, probably working little if at all, without children, and predominantly from two-parent families. Over the past forty years, the college student population has diversified remarkably in terms of gender, race, ethnicity, age, class, ability, and life circumstances. Greater recognition of this diversification has emerged among researchers of college student experience. Perry's work has served as a foundation on which much of this other research on the cognitive development of college students has continued. For example, although Perry's scheme and basic structures have been found to "work" for women, Belenky, Clinchy, Goldberger, and Tarule (1986) found in their research on the cognitive development of a broad range of women (both in and out of college) that Perry's scheme missed some elements of women's development, including such issues as silence, voice, view of self, and relationship to Authority (see Chapter Two). Rodgers (1990) questioned whether these issues of silence, voice, view of self, and relationship to Authority are issues of the epistemological structure of meaning making or, rather, just differences in style.

Finally, attending college in the 1950s was much more an intentional and self-motivated choice than it is today. In his observations about the relationship of motivation to development, Perry (1970) noted that most of his students experienced a quite conscious urge toward maturation. He identified such motivations as sheer curiosity, a striving for competence, an urge to make order out of incongruities, a wish for authenticity in personal relationships, and a wish to develop and affirm an identity. It can be assumed that such motivations exist to at least some degree in college students today (especially in first-generation and older college students). However, given the fact that attending colleges has become a normative expectation and a societal assumption rather than a self-motivated choice, it can perhaps also be assumed that these internal motivations are less pervasive and weaker than in Perry's group of participants. Perry also noted that many of his students did not experience the environment as imposing on them a "press" to mature and, in fact, some experienced a "press" to remain immature. If a decline in self-motivation among college students in general is a valid assumption, then creating environments that induce maturation or growth becomes that much more important. Kuh, Schuh, and Whitt's study of "involving colleges" (1991) bears this out. Their findings include such concerns as the importance of communicating and upholding high expectations for everyone.

Conclusion

William Perry's scheme of cognitive development, though more than thirty years old, is still being used by practitioners today (such as Gallagher, 1998; Kloss, 1994; and Thoma, 1993) to enhance practice in and out of the classroom. It laid a foundation for new research to extend, challenge, and build onto the scheme. The next three chapters review the work of researchers who did just that.

2

In focusing on the cognitive lives of a diverse group of women, Belenky, Clinchy, Goldberger, and Tarule added richness to the growing theory base on college students' cognitive development.

Women's Ways of Knowing

Mary Field Belenky, Blythe McVicker Clinchy, Nancy Rule Goldberger, and Jill Mattuck Tarule studied the ways of knowing of 135 rural and urban women of different ages (from sixteen to over sixty), classes, ethnic backgrounds, and educational histories. Emerging from, inspired by, and drawing on the work of Perry (1970) in cognitive development and of Gilligan (1982) in women's moral and personal development, their work resulted in *Women's Ways of Knowing: The Development of Self, Voice, and Mind* (1986). Their theory described five knowledge perspectives, or frameworks, by which women make meaning of their lives and view themselves and the world (Goldberger, 1997, p. 252). They discovered dimensions and issues that were significant in the narratives of women but were missing from major developmental theories (Goldberger, 1997). Tarule (1997) points out that their findings were gender related but not gender specific. They found that individuals' layered and nested identities were related to the issues of race, class, gender, ethnicity, physical ability, sexual orientation, and regional affiliation, and that all of these issues came into play in the process of cognitive development. Their theory recognized cognitive development as a culturally influenced psychological process (Goldberger, 1997). The work of Belenky, Clinchy, Goldberger, and Tarule represented an important investigation into the processes of cognitive development because it focused on women, social classes, and differences that are significant in our society.

The Five Epistemological Perspectives

True to its subtitle—*The Development of Self, Voice, and Mind*—Belenky, Clinchy, Goldberger, and Tarule's work described cognitive development as dependent on the evolution of identity (self); the interrelationship of the self with others (voice); and the understanding of truth and knowledge (mind) as defined by the self. Like Perry (1970), Belenky, Clinchy, Goldberger, and Tarule (1986) asserted that their epistemological perspectives were not stages. They were not fixed, exhaustive, or universal; the perspectives were abstract and, therefore, did not capture the actual complexity of individuals' lives.

Their five epistemological perspectives were silence, received knowledge, subjective knowledge, procedural knowledge, and constructed knowledge. The remainder of this chapter describes each of the five epistemological perspectives by addressing the concerns of self, voice, and mind. The events and actions that characterize the transition from one perspective to the next are also described.

Silence. Women are often silenced by the culture or by the actions of others, regardless of their epistemological positions. The first position in Belenky, Clinchy, Goldberger, and Tarule's scheme is labeled *silence* because silence was the overwhelming experience of the women who encountered the world from this position. These women were distinguished from other women in the study by their isolation, fearfulness, and acceptance of the status quo. They were without voice and had a very fragile sense of self or mind. As Goldberger (1997) points out, the perspective of silence was not a way of knowing but a way of *not* knowing. The impact of social, economic, and educational forces was highlighted by the fact that not all the women in the study experienced this position—it was not a universal or necessary perspective for cognitive development. Silence was forced on some women by domineering parents, authoritarian spouses or partners, or other authority figures.

The women in this study who viewed the world from the perspective of silence were among the youngest and most socially, economically, and educationally deprived; these women had no college experiences. They exhibited an extreme denial of self and an intense dependence on external authority for direction. Their experience of authority was overwhelmingly negative. They described authorities as all-powerful, overpowering, and unpredictable. What these women tended to have in common was that they grew up in isolation, had few friends, came from families who were cut off from the broader community, and could recall little play or dialogue in the family. These experiences were compounded because most of them had at least one parent who was violent (usually the father) and another parent who was silent and compliant. Women who viewed the world from this position were unable to speak out or protest the sexual and physical abuse they suffered, either as children or in current relationships.

Belenky, Clinchy, Goldberger, and Tarule (1986) described these women as being without voice because they expressed feelings of being deaf and dumb and gave no indication of an internal dialogue with the self. To these women, words were weapons used to separate and diminish people. These women viewed themselves as incapable of knowing or thinking; they could not cultivate their capacities for representational thought, and they thought about life in very concrete ways. Their acts of knowing were limited to the present and to actual, concrete, specific behaviors and concepts. They had no confidence in their ability to learn from experience, and they had no sense of connection with others or with a community.

These women failed to develop their minds, viewed themselves as powerless and dependent, and were passive, incompetent, subdued, and subordinate. Conceptions of the self were linked to actions of knowing and thinking, and therefore there was really no self in silence. Describing any sense of self was nearly impossible for silent women. Their source of self-knowledge was lodged in others, usually in an authority figure. They had no vantage point outside themselves and could not bring their whole self into view. These women lacked the capability and the experience of carrying on a dialogue with others or themselves. They were unaware of the existence of a self and were unable to have an internal dialogue.

Transition to Received Knowing. Across the entire spectrum of epistemological perspectives, most of the women in the study identified experiences that led to significant changes in the way they thought about knowledge, truth, authority, and themselves—experiences that prompted and promoted their development. These transformative and transitional events varied from person to person but included formal education, childbearing, family trauma, difficult or challenging relationships, exposure to other cultures, a new kind of work, or psychotherapy (Goldberger, 1997). For many of the silent women, giving birth was a major turning point in life. For some of the women caught in the web of silence, the event of bringing a child into the world served as the stimulus for moving beyond silence. By giving birth and raising children, women in this position found that they could receive, retain, and pass on knowledge to others (their children), that they had a mind, and that they could communicate (voice).

Received Knowing. The position of received knowing is similar to Perry's dualism in that women in this position perceived authorities as the sole source of Truth—one single Truth. In order to obtain knowledge and truth, received knowers learned through listening to authorities (Belenky, Clinchy, Goldberger, and Tarule, 1986). The practice of receiving, retaining, and imitating the words of authorities was considered the primary task of learning. From the perspective of silence, words were viewed as weapons; in received knowing, words were recognized as vital and central to the learning process. However, given that words (knowledge) could only come from authorities and that the woman was not considered a source of knowledge, a received knower had great difficulty doing original work. To these women, learning was memorizing information, not constructing knowledge.

These women were described as being unable to accept gradations of truth; they perceived no gray areas. To them a paradox was inconceivable, and they found ambiguity intolerable. For instance, these women had trouble understanding poetry because they could not "read between the lines." In class they either did or did not "get" an idea; they did not have the ability to try to "understand" the idea. They could not work from what they already knew and then look for clues and connections to help them understand ideas that they did not know (Belenky, Clinchy, Goldberger, and Tarule, 1986).

Though these women began to develop a voice, they expressed little confidence in their own ability to speak. They learned to emphasize hearing, listening, and receiving. Unlike women in silence, received knowers had a nascent experience of self. However, it often was defined externally. They looked to others for self-knowledge; they still did not see themselves, or their experiences, as legitimate sources of knowledge. Personal power was achieved by identifying with and conforming to social norms, gender roles, and expectations (Goldberger, 1997). Received knowers tended to model themselves after the cultural ideals of what a woman should be, as communicated by church, family, teachers, and other authorities.

A difference emerged, however, between Perry's dualistic men (1970) and women who were received knowers. Perry's dualistic men tended to align themselves with authority (Authority-right-we). On the other hand, women who were received knowers tended to see authority as disconnected and separate from themselves (Authority-right-they). In fact, several of the women indicated that authority figures (typically male college faculty) often communicated to them that women did not belong in college. In some extreme cases, women described experiences where authority figures used their authority to extract sexual favors. These women—whether in or out of college—had few female role models, mentors, or sponsors in traditional authority positions. These women tended to believe that they should devote themselves to the care and empowerment of others while remaining "selfless." They could advance themselves only through helping others.

Transition to Subjective Knowing. It was very difficult for women to remain received knowers in college. The demands of college were counter to the expectations of a received knower; these women either dropped (or were pushed) out or advanced cognitively. Relationships exhibiting mutuality, equality, and reciprocity were most helpful in enabling received knowers to separate their own emerging voice from others and to disentangle their sense of self from the opinions and beliefs others had about them. Experiences resulting in praise and reinforcement also helped transform these individuals. Exposure to a diversity of opinions motivated some of the women to move from a position of received knowing to one in which they relied on themselves as a source of knowledge, which was reminiscent of Perry's observations (1970). The shift from a position of received knowing often had little to do with academic experiences. For women outside the education system, a return to formal education usually *followed* the onset of subjective knowing; formal education did not usher it in.

The shift from received knowing to subjective knowing was more often due to changes in the personal lives of these women. In fact, education tended to be alienating and irrelevant to most of the received knowers. Loss of trust in male authority was the common factor that contributed to this transition. The absence of fathers, the general incompetence of husbands, boyfriends, or bosses, and the experience of violence or sexual abuse at the hands of male authority were all experiences that motivated the change in the women's way of knowing.

Note: At this point, some male readers become alienated from *Women's Ways of Knowing* because they see the work as "male bashing." In their book, Belenky, Clinchy, Goldberger, and Tarule described frankly and clearly the sexual harassment and abuse some participants experienced from the men in their lives. The authors substantiated these findings by citing the research evidence of others regarding the pervasiveness of sexual harassment and abuse in our society. It is important for all student development professionals to be knowledgeable about sexual harassment and sexual abuse and to become self-aware of any discomfort they experience. We hope that you will read on.

Subjective Knowing. In the study, subjective knowing represented a dramatic shift in the experiences of the women. The recognition of the self as an authority was the most dramatic aspect of the shift. Women viewing the world from this perspective now possessed two new and very important elements for the development of "mind" (that is, cognitive development): a "voice" and a "self." The dramatic shift to subjective knowing was composed of many subtle shifts. Instead of seeing oneself as passive, static, and silent, the subjective knower became active and growing and developed a protesting inner voice. Some of these women still may have been silent to the outer world, and all still had a dualistic orientation of right-wrong; but they all experienced a shift in whom they perceived to be right and to whom they listened. In subjective knowing, women became their own authority.

In contrast to the fear and lack of identification with authority that received knowers experienced, women who reached the perspective of subjective knowing became their own authorities and relied first on their own experiences and feelings for knowledge and truth. Belenky, Clinchy, Goldberger, and Tarule (1986) referred to this perspective of knowing as "the infallible gut" and estimated that half of the women in the study were at this stage. This perspective was not tied to any specific age.

For these women, truth was personal, private, and subjectively known; it was experienced, not thought out. Their dominant learning mode was inward listening and watching. They distrusted logic, analysis, abstraction, and even language. Instead, they relied on intuition and the direct perception of truth—independent of any conscious reasoning process. Many distrusted books and the written word, preferring to learn through direct sensory experience and personal involvement. Other people's opinions did not often change the mind of the subjective knower because she was locked inside her own subjectivity; however, like-minded people might be sought out to affirm her opinions (Goldberger, 1997).

Pervasive sexual harassment and abuse was a significant theme in the stories of these women. This abuse had an important influence on the cognitive development of subjective knowers. Of the women interviewed, 38 percent of the college women and 65 percent of the other women had experienced incest, rape, or sexual seduction by a male authority. When this abuse was incestuous, denial and silence carried over into the educational realm and contributed to a lack of trust in male authority and an unwillingness to speak publicly. Authorities, usually female peers and relatives, became personal and private.

Subjective knowing is similar in its emphasis on personal truth to Perry's position (1970) of multiplicity. Perry located the shift to multiplicity in early adolescence, but Belenky, Clinchy, Goldberger, and Tarule (1986) found that the transition to subjective knowing was spread out over the life span of women. This was no surprise because perceiving multiple perspectives was almost unavoidable for advantaged male children, such as those interviewed by Perry and his colleagues. Given their identity with authority (Authority-right-we), males could foresee their own future as authorities. Belenky, Clinchy, Goldberger, and Tarule (1986) identified as "hidden multiplists" women who were advantaged and approached multiplicity with more caution than their male counterparts. Separation and individuation often left hidden multiplists feeling vulnerable and unconnected. Risk taking and stand taking—hallmarks of multiplicity—were not supported in the experiences of these women. Instead, many of them experienced a lifetime of rewards for quiet predictability, obedience, and conformity. Therefore, these female multiplists tended to keep their multiplicity silent. They felt that they should hear people out (because all have a right to an opinion), though, like their male counterparts, they felt under no obligation to accept or agree with the ideas of others. However, this silence also prevented these women from finding mentors or sponsors and led many women to experience college as a stifling, fragmented, and disconnected environment.

The transition to subjective knowing appeared to be a more significant transition for these women than the shift from dualism to multiplicity was for Perry's men. For Perry's men, development emerged from past experiences. For many of these women, however, development could proceed only if they *jettisoned* their past; it was their past, filled with abusive or dead-end relationships, that inhibited their development. In breaking with the past, many embarked on a quest for personal experiences and discovery. For some it took great courage or what they perceived to be recklessness. These women rejected others' claims on them and often removed those claims by leaving their situation or relocating geographically.

Some of the subjective knowers found it difficult to describe themselves in terms of their past, and this disconnection resulted in an unstable sense of self and insecurity for some women. Increased strength, optimism, and self-value also accompanied the growth in subjective knowers. Most subjective knowers were forward looking, positive, and open to new experiences. Unfortunately, some of these women became entrenched in their subjective world and were unwilling to expose themselves to alternative conceptions. The extremely entrenched subjectivist women experienced loneliness, despair, and dead-end isolation; they were cut off from experiences and relationships that might encourage development to a more advanced stage of cognitive development.

Transition to Procedural Knowing. At least two phenomena contributed to the movement beyond subjective knowing. One experience was that these women began to notice inner contradictions through the development and expansion of an inner sense of self, voice, and mind. The other experience was a recognition of their own sense of authority derived from their personal experience. Through observing and reflecting on their experiences, these women began to realize that some of their intuitions and gut reactions were in error, that they could know things they never saw or touched, and that expertise other than their own could be respected. Related to the latter phenomenon was an emphasis on hearing themselves think while gathering observations through watching and listening. This was the precursor to reflective and critical thought. By reaching out to others, these women began to realize that authority and answers could exist beyond their own experience.

Procedural Knowing. Most of the women interviewed who were procedural knowers were privileged, intelligent, white, young (eighteen to twenty-five), homogeneous, and in (or beyond) college. For the procedural knower, there had to be rules and means for discerning the relative worth of authority and the relative truth of knowledge and wisdom—they recognized that they needed procedures for knowing. The move from subjective knowing to procedural knowing was a move from absolutism (subjectivism) to reasoned reflection. However, the first steps away from subjective knowing did not feel like progress because the inner voice of the women turned critical, both toward inner truth and experience and toward external authority. The subjectivist voice diminished in volume while a softer, more active and powerful voice—the voice of reason—became evident.

The emphasis in procedural knowing was on the procedures, skills, and techniques of processing the accuracy of external truth and authority (Belenky, Clinchy, Goldberger, and Tarule, 1986). At that point, forms of thinking and analyzing overshadowed the content of the issue in question. In fact, procedural knowers verged on "methodolatry" (an overemphasis on the means of knowing) to the virtual exclusion of ends. They no longer assumed that all authorities were negative, and they attempted to reach out and understand external authorities. In most cases, especially for the college-going women in the group, authorities were the intellectual elite of their institutions (Goldberger, 1997) who appeared to offer techniques for constructing answers, rather than those who offered absolute answers. These authorities judged the procedures for substantiating their opinions, not their opinions. Using the tools of analysis and critical thinking began as mere "lip service" and parroting. Their experiences were not dissimilar to Perry's emerging relativists who tried to simulate "how to think," not "what to think." There were two interconnected, but distinct, tracks within the perspective of procedural knowing: separate knowing and connected knowing. The following quotes from two women, both college sophomores, represented the two modes of thinking for procedural knowers (Belenky, Clinchy, Goldberger, and Tarule, 1986, p. 100). The separate knower commented, "I never take anything someone says for granted. I just tend to see the contrary. I like playing devil's advocate, arguing the opposite of what somebody's saying, thinking of exceptions to what the person has said, or thinking of a different train of logic." The connected knower approached knowledge differently: "When I have an idea about something, and it differs from the way another person is thinking about it, I'll usually try to look at it from that person's point of view, see how they could say that, why they think they're right, why it makes sense."

One distinction between the two perspectives was related to the concepts of knowledge and understanding. Separate knowers sought knowledge and evaluated knowledge claims via justification (Is it right or wrong?). To have knowledge, one was separated from the object of knowing, the object was evaluated from a distance, and the knower was above the object and had mastery over it. Relationships in separate knowing involved considering the object of knowing from the knower's own standpoint.

Connected knowers sought to go beyond knowledge and tried to understand. Understanding implies a personal acquaintance with and recognition of a relationship to the object. In connected knowing the knower was trying to understand from the perspective of the other—on and in their terms. Connected knowers ask, "Do I understand what you are trying to say?" Belenky, Clinchy, Goldberger, and Tarule (1986) argued that procedural knowers spoke with the voices of both separate and connected knowing.

Separate knowers tended to be at or from traditional, elite, liberal arts colleges. These women refused to adopt the conventional female role. Instead, they became adept at the art of academic knowing, the heart of which was critical and tough-minded thinking. Feelings and personal beliefs were rigorously excluded and repressed in the process of separate knowing (Belenky, Clinchy, Goldberger, and Tarule, 1986; Tarule, 1997). This style of knowing was labeled by Belenky, Clinchy, Goldberger, and Tarule (1986) as "the doubting game." Instead of believing that all people had a right to their own opinion, all knowledge claims were doubted until proven worthy through critical analysis. However, few women interviewed found argument or debate a congenial form of conversation. This style of knowing may represent a public voice encouraged by the academic norms of objectivity, distance, and abstraction (Tarule, 1997). In fact, some of these women saw the skill of critical analysis as empty—a tool to be used but ultimately unsatisfying. It did not really represent who they were. Self (who they were) was still distinct from mind (how they knew).

Connected knowing differed from separate knowing in that connected knowing was built on the conviction that the most trustworthy knowledge came from personal experience (Belenky, Clinchy, Goldberger, and Tarule, 1986). This perspective of knowing also involved procedures, but the procedures for gaining access to other people's knowledge were subtler and less obvious than those employed by separate knowers. Connected knowing was a quest for connection with people and ideas and a projection of self and mind outward to others. It included seeking the context of others' ideas as well as the ideas themselves. This was not the case of one person invading another's mind but of one person opening up mentally to receive another's experience. Rather than the "doubting game" of separate knowing, this was the "believing game": seeing other people's points of view, assuming that there was worth in those points of view, and actively looking for that worth. With a focus on understanding the other, the connected knower was sensitive to the particulars—the context in which the knowledge of others was embedded (Tarule, 1997).

For connected knowers, the conversation to assess the knowledge claims of others was intimate, informal, and unstructured, not impersonal or dictated by formal rules. The conversations of connected knowers were more like clinical interviews rather than the courtroom-style interrogations used by separate knowers. The connected questioner allowed respondents to control and develop their responses to questions. Connected knowing consciously incorporated personal knowledge and helped the other person think the problem through. In connected knowing, authority was derived from the commonality of experience: the greater the connection, the greater the authority among participants. The connected knower began with an attitude of trust, built trust with the other, assumed the person had something worthwhile to say, and refused to rush to judgment about knowledge claims. This style of knowing involved a great deal of patience. As trust developed among the knowers in a relationship of connected knowing, so did the occurrence of criticism. However, the criticism was viewed as supportive, not as an attack on the person or the ideas being presented. Because of the time needed to develop a "connected" environment, a relationship of connected knowing was very hard to accomplish at a typical college. In fact, connected knowers often found the traditional college's academic environment alien and alienating and experienced a sense of disconnection and powerlessness in that context (Tarule, 1997).

Transition to Constructed Knowing. All women who made the transition from procedural knowing to constructed knowing went through a period of intense self-reflection and self-analysis. They described it as turning back on the self—making the self an object of study and sense making. This period of reflection and analysis was prompted by such actions as removing themselves psychologically or geographically from what they knew and lived or, less dramatically, by realizing that reason was necessary but insufficient for knowing or evaluating the knowledge claims of others. They felt a need to integrate thinking with feeling and rationality with emotionality. The women were trying to find a place for reason, intuition, and the expertise of others in the knowing process. Only after a thorough self-examination did the constructed knower recognize the constructed nature of the knowledge, truth, and self that guided their commitments and intellectual and moral life.

Constructed Knowing. Constructed knowing represented an integration of the knower (self), the known (mind), and the communication of the known (voice). The processes of knowing (perspectives) were interconnected and *recognized* as interconnected. The core insights of constructed knowers were that all knowledge was constructed and that the knower was an intimate part of the known. Other fundamental characteristics of constructed knowers were a high tolerance for internal contradiction and ambiguity; a recognition of the inevitability of conflict and stress in the process of constructing knowledge; a recognition of the importance of context in the knowing process; an appreciation for complexity; and a sense of humility about their own knowledge.

Belenky, Clinchy, Goldberger, and Tarule (1986) also found that constructed knowers tended to be articulate and reflective, to notice what was going on with others, and to care about the lives of people around them. They described these women as self-conscious and as being aware of their own thoughts, judgments, moods, and desires. They also indicated that these women participated in what they termed "real talk," which consisted of careful listening, mutual encouragement, exploration of ideas, talking *and* listening, posing questions, arguing, speculating, and sharing. In "real talk," listening no longer diminished the capacity to hear one's own voice. In "real talk," domination was replaced with reciprocity and cooperation.

The constructed knowers in the study recognized that knowledge (and truth) was mutable and in a constant process of construction, deconstruction, and reconstruction. They did not dismiss former ways of knowing because they wanted to stay alert to the fact that different perspectives, and different points in time, produced different answers. Truths even within the self were viewed as mutable—a matter of personal history, circumstance, and timing—and internal truths could conflict and change with time. Answers to all questions varied depending on the context in which they were asked and on the frame of reference of the person doing the asking. Constructivist women were no more immune to the experience of feeling silenced than any other group of women. For some constructivist women (particularly those who did not shy away from speaking their minds) enduring, intimate relationships appeared hard to establish. These women had difficulties finding companionable and supportive men, and they experienced loneliness and discouragement.

Implications for Student Affairs Professionals

Overall implications are addressed in Chapter Seven, but several items specific to the work of Belenky, Clinchy, Goldberger, and Tarule need to be cited here. Although these implications may be applicable to men, given the focus of the research, they are addressed in regard to women.

Recognize the potential need on the part of some women to reject their past.
As previously pointed out, given the predominantly negative experiences in their lives, some women need to jettison their past in order to advance cognitively. Student affairs professionals should be wary of the notion that someone unwilling to "process" the past is in some way emotionally unhealthy. In some cases, this action is quite healthy and needed for further development.

Recognize the role of sexual harassment, abuse, and violence in many women's lives and its subsequent influence on cognitive development.
The subjects of sexual abuse and violence remain taboo in many contexts on college campuses. In order to address cognitive development, student affairs professionals must be aware of and appropriately explore the potential existence of such experiences, especially in their female students who are struggling academically and socially.

Recognize the potential disconnection from authority experienced by some women.
Belenky, Clinchy, Goldberger, and Tarule pointed out that many of the women they interviewed experienced no sense of connection with authority. This disconnection may exacerbate academic problems experienced by some women, given their inability to identify with, and therefore their unwillingness to approach, such authority figures as faculty.

Nurture voices of both separate and connected knowing and the integration of the two.
The tendency on the part of women in this study was to emphasize one voice more than the other in procedural knowing. Some of this preference was due to the environment, such as the tendency for elite liberal arts colleges to nurture and reward separate knowing. Student affairs professionals need to recognize the existence of both voices and try to nurture both in their female students.

Conclusion

What Belenky, Clinchy, Goldberger, and Tarule described resonates with both formal and informal bodies of literature. Their work represents a bridge and a connection between the formal research on cognitive development (such as Piaget and Perry) and the more anecdotal treatises on issues of teaching, learning, and the knowledge inherent in the role of mother (such as Martin, 1985) and in "maternal thinking" (Ruddick, 1980). By interviewing women from a variety of contexts, Belenky, Clinchy, Goldberger, and Tarule presented a process of development that is somewhat less linear and more varied than Perry's. The similarity of the experiences among the participants in Perry's study might be due, in part, to the fact that the participants' context (that is, Harvard) was held constant. Through both the similarities to, and the differences from, Perry's work, Belenky, Clinchy, Goldberger, and Tarule contributed important insights to our understanding of the cognitive development of college students.

Understanding gender-related patterns of knowing and reasoning helps student affairs educators create learning environments that empower students both in and out of the classroom.

Baxter Magolda's Epistemological Reflection Model

Marianne T. Bock

The contributions of Marcia Baxter Magolda to our understanding of the development of complex reasoning among college students continue to foster a professional dialogue about the patterns and processes of cognitive change. Her research on the ways in which students make sense of their educational and learning experiences resulted in an epistemological reflection model that illuminates gender-related patterns of knowing and reasoning in traditional-aged college students.

Baxter Magolda was inspired to conduct her longitudinal study of students' cognitive development because of a need to explain discrepancies between what she observed in students' patterns of cognitive development and William Perry's forms (1970) of intellectual development. Her study extended.Perry's foundational framework and King and Kitchener's reflective judgment model (1981) to focus on gender-related patterns. Her recognition of the similarities between Perry's work and Belenky, Clinchy, Goldberger, and Tarule's theory (1986) of women's ways of knowing provided additional impetus for her to examine gender-related patterns of knowing.

Baxter Magolda (1992) outlines six principles that underlie both the process and the results of her study:

1. The making of meaning is influenced by each individual's worldview and by interaction with others and depends on the context of an individual's experience.
2. Ways of knowing can best be understood through the principles of naturalistic inquiry, which preserve the integrity of individual stories and experiences.

3. Reasoning patterns are not mutually exclusive and may shift in changing contexts and over time.
4. Patterns are related to, but not dictated by, gender.
5. Student stories and interpretations of patterns cannot automatically be generalized to other contexts.
6. Ways of knowing, and reasoning patterns within them, were presented as patterns in order to describe the predominant ways of knowing.

The Study

Baxter Magolda describes her longitudinal study of the cognitive development of male and female college students in *Knowing and Reasoning in College* (1992). Beginning in 1986, 101 students were selected to be interviewed during each year of college. Seventy students were involved for the duration of the five-year study. The students were overwhelmingly white (only 3 of the original 101 were students of color), traditional-aged, and middle class. There were an equal number of men and women, and all of the students were enrolled at Miami University, an academically selective Midwestern university. The students in the study participated regularly in campus organizational and service activities, honors programs, and international study programs; many worked part-time on or off campus.

Baxter Magolda cautions her readers that the three story lines she identified throughout her interviews (voice, relationship to authority, and relationship to peers) may be significantly different for nonmajority students whose socialization and experiences with authority and peers have taken place in different cultural contexts. Dialogue with students from different backgrounds is imperative before determining the transferability of the epistemological reflection model.

Patterns of Knowing

Four knowledge stages that describe the various levels of reasoning exhibited by students are included in Baxter Magolda's epistemological reflection model: absolute knowing, transitional knowing, independent knowing, and contextual knowing. These represent four stages that students experience as their manner of knowing and reasoning changes in conjunction with their overall development and in relationship to the social context of their learning.

Gender-related patterns of reasoning exist within the first three stages; however, Baxter Magolda (1992) indicates that these patterns were not exclusive to each gender; men and women actually exhibited more similarities than differences in their patterns of reasoning. Consequently, the patterns in the model represent "a continuum bounded by a pattern on each end, with numerous variations and combinations in between" (p. 13). Regardless of gender, students seemed to move fluidly within and between reasoning patterns.

Each epistemological stage and gender pattern carries a different set of expectations for the roles of the learner, peers, and instructor; implies appropriate methods of evaluation; and suggests a different view of the nature of knowledge. The underlying assumption that each learner holds about the nature of knowledge helps to illuminate the ways in which they interact with peers and teachers and how they view their role in the learning process.

Absolute Knowing. For the absolute knower, knowledge exists as a certainty and is possessed by certain authorities, specifically teachers. Uncertainty in knowledge exists only when students do not know the correct answer, and any discrepancies between teachers is attributed to varying opinions as opposed to true differences (Baxter Magolda, 1992). Students at this stage see no place for themselves in the creation of knowledge; rather they assume that their role and the role of their peers is to obtain knowledge from teachers. This concept of knowledge leads students to believe that there are correct choices to be made and that, similar to the assumptions of Perry's dualistic thinker (1970), there are right and wrong answers.

The act of learning is seen as a process of collecting information in class and taking it away to learn. Students expect teachers to be able to communicate information in such a way that students will understand it, and they trust that their teachers will be able to judge their learning. While they expect to share material with their peers and to assist each other by explaining what they have learned, they do not expect peers to play a significant role in their learning. Evaluation provides an opportunity for students to demonstrate to the instructor what knowledge they have gained, more as a verification that it is correct than as a means of assessing their understanding.

Absolute knowers are characterized by the gender-related patterns of *receiving* and *mastery.* The receiving pattern of knowing is more frequently characteristic of women whereas the mastery pattern is more often characteristic of men. Both patterns are still grounded in the absolute knowers' concepts of knowledge, with similar expectations of instructors. They differ most notably in their approach to learning, expectations of peers, and purposes of evaluation.

Receiving Pattern. Students exhibiting a receiving pattern take an internal approach to learning. They have few expectations of teachers, engaging them only on a limited basis. They tend to rely on peers for support and to help them feel at ease. They take a more passive stance to learning, believing that their responsibility as learners is to collect information without a critical view and to use evaluation as an expected opportunity to report their knowledge. While they recognize that students may have different opinions about what they are being taught as fact, the absolute nature of those facts remains intact. They assume that difficulty in obtaining knowledge from the instructor is their responsibility to correct by adjusting their manner of listening, note taking, or studying. Knowers who follow a receiving pattern see no role for themselves in the construction of knowledge. Their voices are silent, much like those of the received knowers in the study by Belenky, Clinchy, Goldberger, and Tarule (1986).

Mastery Pattern. Contrary to the receiving pattern's internal approach to learning, the mastery pattern focuses more on a verbal and interactive approach. Knowers who follow a mastery pattern expect that teachers will share their knowledge in an interesting, challenging way and often are critical of those who do not. These students accept mutual responsibility with the teacher for their learning, using exchanges with teachers and peers to demonstrate, test, and strengthen their knowledge.

Their approach to thinking and learning is consistent with the stage of the absolute knower, who views knowledge as certain, but with the added dimension of objective, logical thinking and a view of themselves as autonomous. They are able to engage other students in what might be perceived as competitive activities to demonstrate and to further their understanding without concern for the effects of such exchanges on their relationships. This process of mutual challenges provides further evidence of the importance of achievement in the mastery pattern.

Transition to Transitional Knowing. As the gradual shift into transitional knowing occurs, absolute knowers increasingly begin to view knowledge as uncertain and to recognize the limitations of the knowledge possessed by authorities. Encounters with differing views of teachers and peers facilitate the discovery that knowledge is not absolute. Students' level of connection to authority affects how they confront the limitations and ambiguities inherent in complex ideas. In the mastery pattern, students tend to confront increasing uncertainty by using logic and the knowledge they consider to be certain; in the receiving pattern, students' lack of identification with authority enables them to accept uncertainty more readily. Students' participation in the learning process becomes more active as they move into transitional knowing.

Transitional Knowing. Transitional knowers differ from absolute knowers in terms of their concept of knowledge, view of instructors, and relationships with peers in the learning process. The recognition that some areas of knowledge are certain and some are uncertain creates a need for students to understand complex and conflicting ideas. Hearing others' viewpoints becomes a meaningful way to develop that understanding. Peers can help transitional knowers explore knowledge through active exchanges of such alternative viewpoints.

Students' increased focus on the process of learning, as opposed to information acquisition, is facilitated through instructors' teaching methods and receptiveness to student perspectives and through students' involvement, self-expression, and interaction with peers. Instructors who create opportunities for students to apply their knowledge facilitate further the students' understanding and investment in their educational experiences. Transitional knowers expect the process of evaluation of their work to affirm their individual ideas, experiences, and judgment. Although they recognize that instructors' knowledge at times may be uncertain or limited, these students expect instructors to be able to evaluate their understanding of the material.

Students exhibiting the characteristics of transitional knowing fall somewhere on a continuum of *interpersonal* and *impersonal* gender-related patterns. Women tend to use an interpersonal pattern; men tend to use an impersonal pattern. While students in both patterns recognize that knowledge is partially certain and partially uncertain, their inclination is to resolve the uncertainty of knowledge in different ways, particularly in their interactions with peers.

Interpersonal Pattern. For students exhibiting the interpersonal pattern of knowing, relationships and personal knowledge are central to the learning process. In this pattern, knowers tend to focus more on the uncertain aspects of knowledge and attempt to resolve uncertainty by relying heavily on peers. For the interpersonal knower, peers represent an extension of their own understanding. Peers' views are considered valid in developing that understanding, with the emphasis on collecting rather than challenging those views.

The recognition of the uncertainty of knowledge also opens the door for students to develop their own voices, separate from the authority (that is, the instructor). While rapport with instructors is important, particularly in facilitating students' self-expression, dissension also becomes possible. As in the pattern of received knowers, authorities play a less significant role in the interpersonal knowers' learning processes than do peers. Students view their personal experiences and individual characteristics as important factors in making decisions and resolving uncertainty, and they expect that instructors will value those differences in the evaluation process.

Impersonal Pattern. In the impersonal pattern, knowers extend the focus on mastering knowledge to mastering the process of learning. These students are individually focused, using exchanges with peers only to facilitate their learning process. Although knowers following the impersonal pattern recognize the uncertainty of knowledge, they still rely on instructors and other authorities to resolve that uncertainty and to improve their understanding. Challenges from instructors and challenges from peers, especially in the form of debate or discussion, are welcome learning activities for these students. And whereas for interpersonal knowers such exchanges might result in an adoption of the views expressed by peers, for impersonal knowers those interactions are simply designed to increase students' understanding.

The relationship between authority and voice is different for impersonal and interpersonal knowers. Unlike interpersonal knowers, who maintain some distance from authority and whose voice emerges as a function of that distance, the impersonal knowers identify more closely with authority. As they are transitional knowers, the voice of impersonal knowers is not inhibited by that identification. On the contrary, their voice is actually modeled after their instructors' tendency to question and disagree with students. The element of trust perpetuates a reliance on authority for knowledge that is certain and for resolving knowledge that is uncertain. Impersonal knowers expect outcomes that are more definitive and fairness and objectivity in evaluation.

The essential difference between interpersonal and impersonal knowers is defined by what they value most in the learning process. Impersonal knowers value the challenges to their learning from peers and from authority whereas interpersonal knowers value the relationships with and perspectives of their peers. As transitional knowers, students exhibiting both patterns seek the responsiveness and concern of their instructors, but for different reasons. The interpersonal knowers share their experiences and develop their voice more effectively in a classroom environment where a comfortable rapport exists between student and instructor. The impersonal knower values the climate of debate and questioning created by a concerned instructor.

Transition to Independent Knowing. For both interpersonal and impersonal knowers, this process of engaging with others lays the groundwork for the development and expression of a personal voice, which heralds the move to a level of independent knowing. Any learning opportunities through which students' opinions and experiences are validated are powerful tools in the development of individual voice. However, the process will be somewhat different for interpersonal and impersonal knowers because of the nature of their relationships with authorities and with peers.

As students' individual voices begin to emerge, the disconnection of interpersonal knowers from authority actually facilitates the transition. In addition, because they already seek knowledge from peers, little adjustment in how they perceive others' opinions will be needed. On the other hand, the transition from echoing the voice of authority to expressing their own is more of a struggle for impersonal knowers. Impersonal knowers need to accept themselves and their peers as potential sources of knowledge, equal to authorities, before they can express themselves as independent knowers.

Independent Knowing. The nature of independent knowing lies in students' discovery that most knowledge is uncertain. This fundamental shift alters both the source and process of knowing (Baxter Magolda, 1992). Students recognize that they have the capacity and the right to possess and express knowledge—to think independently. They recognize that they and their peers can assume a position of authority in creating ideas, and they expect their instructors to encourage their thinking and expression. They expect to be evaluated and rewarded based on their independent thinking. The voices of independent knowers are no longer silent or tentative.

Independent knowers have come to value their own and others' opinions, maintaining that all individuals are entitled to their own beliefs. Nevertheless, independent knowers reserve the right to disagree and to make decisions based on their own opinions. Students are able to exchange knowledge with others without pressure to persuade them or to be persuaded by them. They are open to the discrepancies inherent in an uncertain world, accepting all perspectives without critique or scrutiny.

The gender-related patterns present among independent knowers differ primarily in the priorities given to their own and others' thinking. Students who exhibit an interindividual pattern maintain a balanced perspective regarding their own and others' opinions; those who follow an individual pattern place a priority on their own ideas over those of others. Women tend toward the interindividual pattern of thinking, and men tend toward the individual pattern.

Interindividual Pattern. Interindividual knowers use the interchange of their own views and the views of others to clarify and refine their thinking. They attribute discrepancies in knowledge and opinions to differences in interpretation or to individual biases. This tendency to value and utilize peers in the learning process is also exhibited by transitional interpersonal knowers, but with interindividual knowers the intake of others' views and the expression of their own is simultaneous and interactive. Interindividual knowers expect instructors to share their value of the exchange of ideas and to collaborate with students in the evaluation process.

Baxter Magolda (1992) identifies two factors that contribute to a further emergence of personal voice among students using the interindividual pattern. First, the openness of the independent stage diminishes interindividual knowers' concerns about how others perceive them, which enables them to freely express their voice without fear. Second, recognition of the connection between their personal and academic lives helps to clarify and validate their knowing. Baxter Magolda describes this interaction as a "[transformation] into a truly interindividual process because it [makes] possible a dialogue between personal ideas and those held by others" (p. 151). A stronger expression of voice and the corresponding self-confidence also place the interindividual knower on a more equal footing with authority.

Individual Pattern. Individual knowers focus on their own thinking and opinions. They value exchanges with peers, but not for the purpose of adapting to others' views. When faced with disagreement, individual knowers tend to hold fast to their opinions, as opposed to listening to those of their peers. This process of independent thinking actually contributes to the sense making in which students need to engage. Individual knowers expect that classroom discussions and evaluations of their progress will center on the expressions of their thinking processes and on their opinions about the subject matter.

The impact of the strengthened place given to their own voice affects the individual knowers' relationship to authority. The students' opinions are now distinct from that of their instructors or their textbooks, and individual knowers give equal credence to their own knowledge and ideas. The need to have opinions validated by authority no longer exists. Individual knowers also take more active roles in defining learning goals and processes.

The primary distinction between interindividual and individual knowers lies in the nature of their connection to and separation from others, specifically peers and authorities. Baxter Magolda (1992) borrows the terms *communion* and *agency* from Bakan (1966). *Communion* describes connection to others, and *agency* refers to separateness from others. Both individual and interindividual knowers move toward a balance of communion and agency, but in slightly different ways. Individual and interindividual knowers demonstrate increased levels of agency as they formulate their own sources and processes of knowing. Stronger agency also can be seen in the distancing of individual knowers from authority. Movement toward communion occurs in both the interindividual and individual knowers in the form of varying levels of openness to the opinions of others. What distinguishes these patterns from those of the absolute and transitional knowers is the movement toward a balance of communion and agency. This transition to a more integrated way of knowing is manifested in those Baxter Magolda (1992) describes as contextual knowers.

Transition to Contextual Knowing. Students move toward contextual knowing when they learn to apply knowledge and to make judgments within a particular context. The questioning that began in transitional knowing serves as an important foundation for understanding the validity of others' ideas and expertise and for understanding the implications of decisions that are made in a particular context. Educational environments that promote freedom of expression and interdependent relationships between students and teachers facilitate contextual knowing.

Contextual Knowing. The increasing similarities of gender-related patterns that were evident among independent knowers merge for contextual knowers. Although independent thinking is still the defining characteristic of contextual knowers, they tend not to formulate opinions and ideas without considering the context surrounding each issue or piece of knowledge. They no longer accept their own or others' ideas without a more critical analysis. The process of making judgments, and integrating and applying knowledge, within a context is the hallmark of a contextual knower. Although this level of thinking is seldom seen among college students (Baxter Magolda, 1992), educators attempting to develop it will encourage critical analysis of problems, ideas, and perspectives.

The relative value that contextual knowers place on the ideas of others is dependent on evidence appropriate to the context. Contextual knowers engage peers and teachers with contextual expertise in exchanging ideas and views to validate their knowledge. Educators who encourage this exchange and who provide opportunities for students to apply their knowledge contribute to the students' decision-making ability and to the development of what one of the participants termed *"self-responsibility* within community" (Baxter Magolda, 1992, p. 188). Contextual knowers engage in a complex process of integrating their own voices with knowledge considered valid in a given context. Their capacity to articulate and apply their knowledge determines their ability to make important contributions to the ongoing construction of human communities.

Baxter Magolda continues to explore the development of contextual knowing among participants in their postgraduate years and to campaign for changes in educational practice that will be responsive to students' learning needs (Baxter Magolda and Terenzini, 1999). Through subsequent research on students' ways of knowing, Welte (1997) pointed out limitations she perceived in the model Baxter Magolda (1992) articulated. Welte suggested that students may use multiple patterns of knowing and reasoning depending on the context; that educators' ways of knowing and the nature and level of each course influence the learning context; and that changes in students' ways of knowing are more frequent and fluid than is reflected in the annual snapshots of their progress. Although Baxter Magolda addressed these issues to some extent, Welte's analysis reminds us to consider the influences of context, our own ways of knowing, and the dynamic combination of students' ways of knowing with our own.

Application of the Model to Student Affairs

The area of career services is one functional area where understanding the processes of knowing and reasoning is important to facilitate the career development process of students. Career counseling staff can gain valuable insights into the career decision making of students by using the stages associated with the epistemological reflection model.

When applying this model to assess the students' career decision making, it is important to recognize that Baxter Magolda's stages are not necessarily associated with class standing or age. She did, however, identify that absolute knowing is more prevalent in the freshman year and transitional knowing is most prevalent in the junior and senior years. Counselors need to focus on assessing each student's progress individually and tailor career recommendations and interventions appropriately.

That being said, traditional-aged freshmen seeking career development counseling often have the characteristics of absolute knowers. Absolute knowers tend to view their career adviser as the authority on all things related to career and the world of work. Counselors will recognize them by the way they seek career information and by the way they make career decisions. They come to the career center expecting to find all of the answers and for the counselor to tell them "what they should be when they grow up." And when they return to their residence hall or classes, they share materials and information that they have received with their peers without much depth of discussion about their experience. They expect the counselor to communicate career information and point them in the appropriate direction. If you ask them what they know about the world of work, they give you cursory information based on their personal experience without any evaluative perspective. Based on that personal experience they eliminate a number of careers without an examination of how those careers might suit them.

At this stage, knowers who follow a receiving pattern accept information from the authority figure without talking with peers beyond informal discussions to ease their tension about the whole process. Knowers who follow a mastery pattern are anxious to gain acceptance from the counselor, to demonstrate their knowledge, and to elicit more knowledge from the counselor. As students develop their own voice and as they progress to new levels of thinking and interacting, their relationship with their counselors and with their peers will change.

As students begin to experience transitional knowing, their level of understanding (beyond just obtaining knowledge) begins to emerge. In making career decisions, they begin to have a greater sense of how they might fit within certain professions and of the implications of certain careers on their lifestyle. Formal assessment instruments that evaluate everything from their "type" (Holland, 1985; Myers, 1980) to their occupational preferences (such as the Kuder Preference Inventory and the California Occupational Preference System), and informal explorations of their interests, abilities, aptitudes, and personality, begin to give them insights and self-awareness and to help them evaluate and compare career choices. They now begin to question the certainty of the knowledge they have obtained and recognize that "drive-in" career counseling is not possible. Their exchanges with peers develop into more in-depth discussions. Interpersonal knowers begin to distance themselves from their counselor and turn more frequently to peers for interaction. Impersonal knowers tend to engage their peers in debates to test their knowledge and understanding. The counselor's job is to assess students' understanding of themselves and of their career options and to prepare them to move forward in the process.

As students move into independent knowing, they start to take the knowledge and understanding they have gained and formulate their own opinions, share their points of view with their peers, and express their initial decisions to their counselor. They expect the counselor to help them apply what they have learned about themselves and their options toward the development of a career plan. Their reliance on the career counselor as *the* authority has diminished, but interindividual knowers may seek to maintain that connectedness with counselors and peers. These knowers tend to seek ways to legitimize their own voice through this connectedness. Individual knowers, on the other hand, rely on others only to help them solidify their own views. Counselors will more likely see independent thinking in upperclassmen although it is not impossible for new students to exhibit independent thinking.

As students prepare to develop their own career plan (a plan that involves more specificity than just selecting a major), it may be a signal to the counselor that the students have moved into contextual knowing. They are more fully aware of how their career decisions and job search strategies will fit into the context of their personal lives. They see the processes of work and life as intertwined and begin to understand and use their own capacity to contribute to others' knowing and understanding. They have successfully integrated their self-knowledge with career options, at least well enough to know where their path will take them initially. They feel free to express their own voice about their career aspirations, and if they have successfully developed an appropriate level of autonomy (Chickering and Reisser, 1993), they can move forward with confidence about their career plan. They view their opportunities in the larger context of a world that is impacted by the economy, politics, and culture; and they know that each career decision, change, or goal will be a reflection of those forces.

This discussion, along with the original research by Baxter Magolda, is focused primarily on the experiences of traditional, fairly homogeneous groups of students. Therefore, it is important to recognize that the process will differ for students of nontraditional age and for minority students. Implications of culture, maturity, and life position also must be taken into consideration. In addition, it is important for the counselor to recognize that the understanding of self and career for each student is something the student will construct jointly with the counselor, peers, and others. The understanding of self and career is a dynamic process that is impacted by students' epistemological position, as well as by their social and emotional development processes. Career counselors must know about developmental processes and be able to use their knowledge to guide students through career selection and planning.

Conclusion

The preceding example of Baxter Magolda's model emphasizes the importance of the patterns of knowing used by students and how important those patterns are to the creation of learning environments that empower students both in and out of the classroom. Based on her findings, Baxter Magolda (1992) recommends that educators make every effort to validate students as knowers, situate learning in the students' experiences, encourage the processes of jointly constructed knowledge, and facilitate learning relationships that empower students.

According to Baxter Magolda and Terenzini (1999), the changing nature of the educational process makes it imperative for educators to be conscious of their assumptions about learning and knowing and to be willing to change those assumptions. In their essay for the American College Personnel Association trends analysis project, they emphasize that "conventional assumptions about students, the collegiate experience, learning, teaching, and assessment will not serve higher education in the 21st century" (Baxter Magolda and Terenzini, 1999, p. 23). Understanding patterns of cognitive development is one critical element in transforming our assumptions and our practice.

MARIANNE T. BOCK is a doctoral fellow in higher education and student personnel at Kent State University.

4

*King and Kitchener's model of reflective judgment pro-
vides a framework for educators to help students enhance
their problem-solving ability by learning to make defensible judgments about vexing problems.*

King and Kitchener's Reflective Judgment Model

Patricia King and Karen Kitchener's book *Developing Reflective Judgment:
Understanding and Promoting Intellectual Growth and Critical Thinking in
Adolescents and Adults* (1994) is based on theory building and research on
the Reflective Judgment Model that began in the mid-1970s. Interviews with
over seventeen hundred people conducted by King, Kitchener, and colleagues form the foundation of the model and have contributed to its recognition among models of cognitive growth as "perhaps the best known and
most extensively studied" (Pascarella and Terenzini, 1991, p. 123).

King and Kitchener's interest in the nature of intellectual development
was inspired when they were doctoral students by a graduate seminar on college student development that focused on William Perry's scheme (1970) of
the intellectual and ethical development of college students. The Reflective
Judgment Model evolved based on King and Kitchener's belief that Perry's
scheme was incomplete in that some individuals reason with assumptions that
are beyond the relativistic positions defined by Perry. In their view, Perry's last
three positions ("commitment in relativism") describe personal commitments
that indicate identity development and individual ethics or values, not the
individual's continued cognitive development. In contrast, the last two stages
of the Reflective Judgment Model "represent the most advanced sets of
assumptions identified to date that are used in solving ill-structured problems"
(King and Kitchener, 1994, p. 17). Hofer and Pintrich (1997, p. 100) concur
that the "central contribution of [King and Kitchener's model] is the theoretical elaboration of the structural and epistemological aspects of the upper levels of Perry's original scheme."

The Reflective Judgment Model was also influenced by John Dewey's
work (1933) on reflective thinking and by the work of developmental the-

orists such as Jean Piaget (1969; Piaget and Inhelder, 1971) and Lawrence Kohlberg (1969), who examined how and why different forms of reasoning evolve. Many of the assumptions on which the Reflective Judgment Model is based are drawn from the work of these theorists; it is thus a stage model description of a cognitive process that is explicitly developmental and constructivist in its orientation. Its stages have an underlying organization, are qualitatively different, and appear to form an invariant sequence.

The Theory

The Reflective Judgment Model describes the development of reflective thinking, an aspect of critical thinking that distinctively focuses on ill-structured problems. Ill-structured problems are complex and controversial problems that are vexing and for which a solution cannot be known with completeness, certainty, or correctness. The basis of this model is seven distinct sets of epistemic assumptions and concepts of justification, or, put more simply, seven consistent patterns that describe how people approach complex issues and defend what they believe to be true. The model is applicable to individuals from late childhood through adulthood. It describes the process by which individuals develop an increasingly better ability to "evaluate knowledge claims and to explain and defend their points of view on controversial issues" (King and Kitchener, 1994, p. 13).

Stage-related assumptions underlie the Reflective Judgment Model. Though the authors use the term *stage* with some qualification, each of the seven stages of the Reflective Judgment Model is internally coherent, and later stages build on earlier ones. Reflective judgment is the outcome of this developmental progression, with each stage representing a more complex and effective form of justification. Although individuals may progress at different rates and as a result of varied experiences, they develop the different forms of thinking in an invariant sequence. Individuals cannot comprehend the meaning of higher stages unless they fully comprehend the meaning of the preceding stages (Kitchener, Lynch, Fischer, and Wood, 1993).

There are many journal articles and book chapters that summarize the model and research associated with it; however, none approaches the breadth and depth of King and Kitchener's *Developing Reflective Judgment* (1994). This comprehensive text uses interview excerpts to illustrate the stages, contains a comprehensive review of the research through 1993, and addresses educational implications of the model. King and Kitchener. "present impressive evidence that students change over time. . . . making our role in higher education paramount in facilitating reflective reasoning" (Liddell, 1995, p. 95). The data suggests that the functional level of most undergraduate students is between stages 3 and 4. However, they may be able to comprehend stage 5 concepts, a feasible optimal level for undergraduates to achieve if they are given opportunities to practice and receive clear feedback about the nature of their performance.

Importance of the Model

According to Liddell (1995, p. 94), "The importance of the reflective judgment model (RJM) and its assessment rests in the questions that academics and practitioners pose about the effectiveness of their teaching, their programs, and their interventions: Am I doing all that I can to help students think in more complex ways and to reason more reflectively?" Enhanced problem-solving ability is the result of engaging in reflective thinking, which culminates in reflective judgment (King and Kitchener, 1994). King and Kitchener (1994, p. 1) assert that "one of the most important responsibilities educators have is helping students learn to make defensible judgments about vexing problems." This certainly applies to learning both in and outside the classroom and suggests that fostering reflective judgment is a legitimate concern and priority for faculty and student affairs educators alike.

The Seven Stages of Reflective Judgment

In describing the seven stages of the model, King and Kitchener have grouped the stages together into three general levels of development: pre-reflective, quasi-reflective, and reflective. In this section, the three general levels and the transitions between these levels are first described to provide a framework of understanding on which to build the more specific discussion of the individual stages.

First Level: Pre-reflective. Individuals reasoning at this level (stages 1, 2, and 3) do not find ill-structured problems particularly perplexing because they do not acknowledge, or perhaps even perceive, knowledge to be uncertain. They assume a correct answer either exists or will exist (though it may have to be discovered through a process of finding the right facts). Knowledge comes directly from authority figures or from the individual's own direct, personal observation; knowledge is thus seen as correct and certain.

Transition to the Second Level. The transition from pre-reflective thinking to the quasi-reflective level may be prompted when individuals face discrepant data that they can no longer deny. When those at the pre-reflective level experience diversity of opinion, different points of view, or differences in culture, their framework for sense making is challenged. The resulting dissonance may force them to seek answers elsewhere, and they may begin to move toward quasi-reflective thinking. A dawning recognition that there are true problems for which there are currently no absolute answers creates confusion. "In the admission that in some cases knowledge is temporarily uncertain lies the potential for recognizing that uncertainty is an inherent part of the process of knowing" (King and Kitchener, 1994, p. 57).

Second Level: Quasi-Reflective. Individuals reasoning at this level (stages 4 and 5) recognize elements of uncertainty and see some situations as truly problematic. They cannot solve ill-structured problems and will argue that it is not possible to make a judgment in these arenas. As King and Kitchener (1994, p. 4) explain, "one simply has an opinion, and one cannot evaluate the strengths or weaknesses of an opinion." Knowledge is seen as ultimately subjective. The notion that judgments ideally should be based on evidence begins to be acknowledged. However, individuals who hold quasi-reflective assumptions are only able to evaluate evidence in an individualistic and idiosyncratic way. Developing and justifying a position on an issue is not yet fully differentiated from merely asserting a position.

Transition to the Third Level. Holding unjustified beliefs in light of being asked for justification creates a dissonance that may lead an individual to seek a clearer relationship between evidence and belief. An initial step may be the acknowledgment that giving reasons for beliefs is an essential part of an argument. Inherent contradictions in their own thinking force quasi-reflective thinkers to seek new ways to justify their knowing and resolve these contradictions. As individuals begin to be able to relate evidence and arguments to knowing, they also begin to accept knowledge as contextual. The need to be able to compare and contrast evidence and to make judgments that remain valid in different contexts prompts the formation of reflective thinking.

Third Level: Reflective. At this level (stages 6 and 7), although individuals can never be certain that their judgments about ill-structured problems are true or correct, they are able to come to defensible conclusions about these complex problems. They acknowledge the uncertainty of knowing, but they believe that a judgment can be constructed by integrating available evidence that is reasonably certain and expert opinion into a reasonable conjecture. At this level, interpretations or knowledge claims can be evaluated; some are seen as more plausible or reasonable than others. Individuals recognize their role as active agents in constructing their understanding of the world and realize that knowledge must be understood in relationship to the context in which it was produced.

Though these three levels are helpful in understanding the theory, the basic components of the Reflective Judgment Model are the seven stages. Each is described below with an example (when appropriate) of how a college student might reason about a typical issue using thinking that is characteristic of that stage.

Stage 1. Stage 1 is characterized by a very simple belief system that consists of only one category: I believe only what I have seen and thus know to be true. It is the "epitome of cognitive simplicity" (King and Kitchener, 1994, p. 50). Knowledge is seen as absolute, and thus controversies do not exist. Legitimate alternatives do not exist. When an individual using these assumptions is faced with discrepant data, the discrepancies are denied. There is no perceived need for, or value in, examining the reasons for holding the belief.

According to King and Kitchener (1994, p. 48), "because reasoning is so concrete, it is difficult to provide examples of reasoning about knowledge at this level since knowledge itself is an abstract concept." In fact, this level has been observed only occasionally in reflective judgment research, and then only in the youngest high school samples. It is probably typical only of young children. Stage 1 assumptions are challenged when the individual experiences diversity (of opinion, point of view, religion, culture). It is the admission of alternatives that paves the way for progression to the next stage.

Stage 2. At stage 2, individuals believe a true reality that can be known with certainty exists but perhaps is not known by everyone. Authorities certainly know the truth, and those who disagree with them are just plain wrong. Because most issues are seen to have a right answer and because there is a right way to believe, individuals reasoning with these assumptions have little conflict in making decisions about what to believe. The assumptions of this stage have much in common with Perry's dualism (1970). Though absolute knowledge is still believed to exist, alternative views are acknowledged and can be classified as right or wrong. In many instances, beliefs are unexamined and unjustified. When they are justified, it is by their correspondence with the beliefs of an authority figure. If evidence is considered at all, it may be distorted to align with beliefs. With this stage comes the appearance of dogmatism and a great deference to authority as the basis for belief. The assumptions at this stage are still too simplistic to allow for an understanding of ill-structured problems but provide a necessary prerequisite in that differences of opinion are perceived.

EXAMPLE. *When I first came to college, I believed that I should major in engineering, as indicated by the interest inventory my high school guidance counselor gave me. After speaking to a college career counselor, who is obviously more qualified to provide this type of advice, I know I should change my major to accounting. I'm glad it didn't take me long to get on the right track.*

Stage 3. Knowing in this stage advances to include the acknowledgment that authorities may not currently have the truth in all areas. However, it is held that at some future point, the truth will be discernible. For the moment there is no way to justify knowledge claims in these areas, and personal opinion or what "feels right" may dictate beliefs. The category of "temporary uncertainty" provides an answer for diverse points of view and discrepant data. People can "believe what they want to believe" in the areas where authorities do not yet know the truth. Evidence for beliefs starts to come into play, but it must point directly to the right answer and cannot be open to interpretation. When individuals use the assumptions of this stage and are asked to make decisions about complex problems, they often appear confused and are unable to coordinate belief and evidence to justify their stances. However, in the recognition of temporary uncertainty lies the potential for recognizing that uncertainty is an inherent part of the process of knowing. Thus, this stage represents an important advancement in the development of reflective judgment.

EXAMPLE. *I was stopped between classes today by a reporter from the college newspaper and asked whether a proposed new college regulation would benefit students. How am I supposed to know that? No one will know the effect on students for years—long after I've graduated! So I don't know. I think I'll find out how my housemates feel about it before I sign the petition for or against. . . . or maybe I just won't sign at all.*

Stage 4. At this stage individuals come to believe that one cannot know with certainty about many issues. In previous stages assumptions have been grounded in concrete constructs; at this stage knowledge and justification are understood as abstractions that are not yet fully related to each other. Therefore, knowing to some degree is idiosyncratic to the individual. Opinions come to be seen as an insufficient basis for developing an argument, but evidence is not yet consistently used. Giving reasons begins to be seen as an essential part of any argument; but these reasons cannot be evaluated, nor can the evidence on which they are based. In many cases evidence is chosen specifically because it validates prior beliefs. If evidence contradicts a particular belief, the belief can still be held with no attempt to resolve the contradiction.

Individuals arguing from a stage 4 perspective may claim to know what is right for them but are frequently unwilling to evaluate or judge others' behaviors or ideas. This stage represents a very important step in the process because knowing must be understood as an abstraction before it can be grasped as a process and linked with justification.

EXAMPLE. *There must be as many "clinical studies" that say that clove cigarettes are bad for you as there are that show no harmful effects. I've never met anybody who ever knew anyone who developed cancer or health problems from smoking just clove cigarettes, so I think the studies that show they are harmful are just trying to scare us into not smoking at all. Until someone proves something for sure or something happens to someone I know who smokes them, I'm going to keep on believing the reports that say they're okay. Everyone just has to decide for him- or herself, "This is what's right for me."*

Stage 5. The primary belief of stage 5 is that "while people may not know directly or with certainty, they may know within a context based on subjective interpretations of evidence, a belief sometimes called relativism" (King and Kitchener, 1994, p. 62). The perceptions and perspectives of the person making the interpretation determine what is known. Therefore, knowledge is contextual and subjective. An awareness develops that different perspectives are based on different types of evidence or varying interpretations of the evidence. At this stage, the ability to relate, compare, and contrast two abstractions is developed. This allows evidence and arguments to be related to knowing. However, the ability to coordinate them into a well-reasoned argument is not yet developed, nor is the ability to compare and contrast evidence across contexts.

EXAMPLE. *I can see that from his perspective as a more science-oriented individual, he believes sexual orientation appears to have a biological or genetic cause. And he has the studies to back up his beliefs. Well, that's his interpretation. I base my opinion on the studies I've read, which point to the importance of environment and indicate that there may be an element of individual choice involved. This fits with my religious beliefs and the experience of those homosexuals I've read about or seen on TV who have changed their sexual orientation or chosen to be a certain way.*

Stage 6. At stage 6, knowing is a process requiring the individual's active involvement. Solutions to ill-structured problems must be *constructed*—even by experts. In other words, complex problems "require some kind of thinking action before a resolution can be constructed" (King and Kitchener, 1994, p. 67). Individuals who reason using stage 6 assumptions report that, to come to a stance on an issue, they look at different perspectives, identify the common elements, and form a new perspective by integrating these elements.

Knowledge is viewed as largely uncertain, and it can only be understood in relationship to context and evidence. Criteria for the evaluation of judgments and beliefs, such as the plausibility of an argument or the utility of a solution, begin to emerge. Knowing and justification are coordinated, which makes possible the comparison and relation of two different views of the same issue. Though evaluations of right and wrong are not frequently made, one view can be held as better than another in that it is based on stronger evidence or is more compelling or appropriate for the situation. The opinions of authorities begin to be considered in a different light: they are now seen as "experts who have investigated the issue more thoroughly or who have special competencies" (King and Kitchener, 1994, p. 68). Authorities' opinions can be differentiated from opinions made by laypeople. However, at this stage conclusions tend to be narrower in scope because a larger system of knowing, allowing comparisons and conclusions across domains, has not yet been constructed.

EXAMPLE. *I have been trying to decide whether spending a term studying abroad or doing an internship would be a better preparation for my career in international business. I respect the opinions of my professors, but they don't all agree. One faculty member in particular has more credibility in my mind because she is more current with job market trends and has even done some research in this area. She thinks a term abroad would be better for me, so I'm leaning toward her advice. I've done some investigating on my own through*

Career Services and learned more about the value of a term abroad, so I'm planning to do this. I think it stands to benefit me careerwise and also in terms of my personal development, which will serve me well in the future no matter what job I wind up doing.

Stage 7. The most complex of all the stages, stage 7 is the most difficult to describe. It is characterized by the belief that although an absolute reality cannot be assumed, one can synthesize interpretations of evidence and opinion into reasonable, cohesive, and justifiable conjectures. This requires critical inquiry where the individual is actively involved in constructing knowledge. It is believed that based on available evidence the process of inquiry will lead to the most complete, plausible, or compelling solutions for ill-structured problems. Once a solution has been constructed, there is an awareness that time, experience, or new data may necessitate new constructions or understandings. "At the same time, [individuals] are able to claim that the conclusions they are currently drawing are justifiable, believing that other reasonable people who consider the evidence would understand the basis for their conclusions" (King and Kitchener, 1994, p. 70).

Grounds for justifying beliefs at this stage include: "the weight of the evidence, the explanatory value of the interpretation, the risk of erroneous conclusions, the consequences of alternative judgments, and the interrelationships of these factors" (King and Kitchener, 1994, p. 72). Stage 7 goes beyond stage 6 in that a general framework about knowing and justification is developed that allows for a generalization of assumptions and greater clarity of judgment. Stage 7 displays intelligent, reflective choice; judgment that in King and Kitchener's words (1994, p. 71) "demonstrates individuality constrained by reason"; and a willingness to critique and reevaluate one's own reasoning.

EXAMPLE. I've done a lot of thinking about this issue and am pretty confident on what I believe to be true. The issue of whether a black cultural center or a multicultural center would better serve the needs of students on this campus is one that can be viewed from multiple perspectives. As African American Graduate Association president, I've had to take a leadership role in this controversy. At first, I think I was seeing things through a fairly narrow perspective. Even now, I know that my own cultural lenses constrain, to some degree, how I am able to see the situation. Further, I know that next term's courses on the psychology of multiculturalism and professional ethics may give me further information and cause me to reevaluate my views. But I've worked hard to construct a full understanding of the ramifications of both options, and I've evaluated the diverse perspectives that have been voiced on the issue. At this juncture I am confident that I have a well-founded position from which I can provide the leadership needed to move forward in AAGA's advocacy position for the students we serve.

Developing Reflective Judgment

It is important to remember that according to this model, individuals are not thought to be at a single point on a developmental scale or "in a stage." Rather, their thinking can be characterized by a developmental range made up of several stages within which they may operate. The developmental range is thought to be bounded by an optimal level (the upper limit of complexity at which the person is able to reason) and a functional level (typical operating level). The type of response an individual uses depends a great deal on prior experience, task demands, personal factors (emotional preoccupations, anxiety, fatigue), and the particular assessment environment in which an individual is operating. Therefore, it is important not to make the assumption that individuals function in a single stage at a given point of time under all circumstances.

In addition, periods of relatively fast growth, or "spurts," tend to mark the emergence of a new developmental stage. Spurts are generally followed by plateaus, during which the new cognitive structure is elaborated and generalized to new areas. Reflective judgment develops as a result of "an interaction between the individual's conceptual skills and environments that promote or inhibit the acquisition of these skills" (King and Kitchener, 1994, p. 18). Spurts in performance typically occur when optimal environmental conditions induce and support them. This may include opportunities to practice and master the skill, active encouragement, training, or other forms of contextual support. Under supportive conditions, students may perform at one stage or more higher than their functional level of reasoning. Unfortunately, according to King and Kitchener (1994, p. 35), "Under ordinary circumstances, most environments do not provide cues or support for high-level performance, especially not about issues of knowing. As a result, people do not typically perform at their optimal level but at their lower, functional level. Improvement in functional level is usually slow and gradual, with performance remaining far below optimal level and varying widely across domains."

Implications for Student Affairs Educators

Student affairs educators work with students in residential living environments, student organizations, committees, courses (such as freshman seminars and leadership courses), and other situations that bring them into close and sustained contact. King and Kitchener (1994) note that sustained contact and a trusting relationship are essential for determining what skills a student can use under optimal conditions. A wide variety of educationally purposive interactions with students can be intentionally used to foster reflective thinking in college students. Our challenge is to stimulate students to ask more complex questions and make more effective judgments on the complex issues they face.

In working with undergraduate students, student affairs educators can generally focus on promoting development between the pre-reflective and quasi-reflective levels (more specifically, between stages 3 and 4). First-year college students typically have been assessed at 3.5 on the Reflective Judgment Interview (RJI), with only one sample of academically talented college freshmen averaging above 4.0 (King and Kitchener, 1994). The highest average mean score for college students was 5.0, which was found among seniors. King and Kitchener (1994, p. 225) report, "every senior sample had an RJI mean score of over 3.5, and half were over 4.0. The average score for seniors was 4.00, making the average freshman-senior difference about half a stage." This small numerical difference represents a noteworthy development in reasoning that is described by Kroll (1992) as the abandonment of "ignorant certainty" in favor of "intelligent confusion." It is with this movement that students come to acknowledge that uncertainty is not just a temporary condition of knowing. They move away from the absolutism of pre-reflective thinking into a level that prepares them for truly reflective thinking. Also, at this level, evidence is used to support judgments—a crucial foundational skill for making reflective judgments.

The goals and strategies adopted to encourage reflective thinking should be appropriate for students' level of reasoning and include both challenges and supports for the development process (Sanford, 1962). Activities designed to engage students in new ways of thinking are generally challenging and should be balanced with "a supportive foundation so that students will risk using those higher-level reasoning skills that feel unfamiliar or that introduce doubt and perplexity" (Sanford, 1962, p. 244). Interesting and engaging topics, tasks for which students have the necessary background and skills, and methods for legitimizing students' discomfort and providing encouragement are supports in interactions with students. It is also important to remember that what students perceive as challenges and supports can differ greatly by developmental level.

Ill-structured problems exist in many different areas of student life and student affairs work. Which student leader would make the most effective organizational president? Is a particular policy going to benefit the students and have a positive developmental impact? Which candidates should be chosen as resident assistants? How should funding be allocated among the student organizations? These questions are not beyond the understanding of most college students, and grappling with these issues can produce growth. Students need to be exposed to these issues and encouraged to wrestle with these decisions and their implications. It is also important that student affairs professionals give students feedback about their arguments, offer schemata for how to evaluate the adequacy of arguments, and model more advanced reasoning about complex issues.

Students need opportunities and incentives to practice looking at an issue from a variety of perspectives. "In creating such opportunities," King and Kitchener (1994, p. 237) point out, "educators should recognize that some students will need more encouragement than others to suspend judgment while becoming informed about a variety of perspectives." Particular attention should be focused on encouraging consideration and analysis of the evidence used and emphasized by each perspective. Students also should be encouraged to develop and practice strategies for presenting information and ideas from a variety of perspectives. This is particularly crucial for student leaders who are charged with making certain that different views are accurately represented.

Valuable opportunities to observe and practice reflective thinking and to make judgments about vital real-life issues are available through involvement in decision-making bodies such as student governing boards, departmental or campus committees, or advisory councils. Students can be assisted to "critique more actively and adequately the reasoning they see and hear so that they can begin to understand the issues they face from a more informed position" (King and Kitchener, 1994, p. 238). Opportunities for students to make judgments and explain what they believe are particularly powerful developmentally. Students need practice in making, defending, and evaluating their own judgments based on "more than prior belief or peer pressure" (King and Kitchener, 1994, p. 239). This may be overly challenging in large or public settings, but it can also take place in small groups or decision-making bodies, such as screening committees, student-funding boards, and judicial boards.

Student affairs educators have multiple and varied contacts with students that provide rich opportunities to encourage students to make reasoned judgments. The *Principles of Good Practice in Student Affairs*, jointly endorsed by the American College Personnel Association and the National Association of Student Personnel Administrators (1997), defines good practice in student affairs as that which both engages students in active learning, and sets and communicates high expectations for student learning. Creating environments and experiences that support and encourage intellectual development through fostering reflective judgment is at the heart of student affairs work.

*Often overlooked by practitioners are interpersonal, cul-
tural, and emotional influences on the cognitive development of college students.*

Interpersonal, Cultural, and Emotional Influences on Cognitive Development

Although none of the theories reviewed in this book completely ignore the influence of social, cultural, or emotional factors on the process of cognitive development, the traditional view of cognitive development has been individualistic. The individual was studied in isolation, or developmental processes were isolated from context and interactions (Rogoff, 1990). The purpose of this chapter is to highlight social, cultural, and emotional influences because they often become lost when complex theories of cognitive development are summarized. The tendency to ignore social and affective dimensions of cognitive development is further exacerbated by the Western tradition of treating thinking and feeling as mutually exclusive (Clinchy, 1996). The first two sections of this chapter explore the social and societal influences on cognitive development. The first of these sections explores interpersonal influences (the microsocial level) and the second describes the cultural influences (the macrosocial level). The third section of the chapter delineates affective and emotional influences on cognitive development.

Interpersonal Influences on Cognitive Development

The strongest statements related to social and affective influences on cognitive development have been made about the connection between social processes and cognitive development (for example, Baxter Magolda, 1992, 1995; Chickering and Reisser, 1993; King and Baxter Magolda, 1996). Vygotsky (1978) argued that social interaction was not just a facilitator of cognitive development but absolutely necessary and that interpersonal dialogue and interaction were precursors to inner speech and an awareness of one's own thought processes. Belenky, Clinchy, Goldberger, and Tarule

(1986) recognized this dynamic in the women who viewed their world from the position of silence. These women did not have the experience of meaningful dialogue, and this void obstructed their cognitive development. Chickering and Reisser (1993) pointed out that relationships provide powerful learning experiences and opportunities to enhance cognitive development. These relationships include out-of-class faculty-student interaction, which consistently has been shown to be very influential in student growth and outcomes (Astin, 1993; Pascarella and Terenzini, 1991); pedagogical interactions between faculty and students (Brophy, 1985; Good, 1987); social and academic interactions among students (Bean and Creswell, 1980; Harnett, 1965; Kuh, 1995; Weinstein, 1989); and students' perceptions of an instructor's social and academic behaviors (Weinstein, 1989).

In general, current researchers have found it difficult to separate cognitive skills from social processes. In fact, the entire area of research now known as social cognition is premised on the belief that learning occurs in a social context and that one's ability to interact effectively with others requires some level of cognitive ability (and vice versa). Rubin and Henzl (1984, p. 264) maintained that "A cognitively complex individual is better able to adapt to the demands of changing social situations than is a less complex individual. . . . Cognitively complex persons are more skilled at taking the other's perspective and, therefore, should be more effective in sending and receiving messages." Rogoff (1990) viewed cognitive development as an apprenticeship experience where the individual's development is inseparable from interactions with more skilled others, such as peers, adults, faculty, and student affairs professionals. She argued that the individual, social partners, and the cultural milieu are inseparable contributors to the ongoing activities in which cognitive development takes place. She used the analogy of apprenticeship to focus on how the development of cognitive skill involves active learners observing and participating in organized cultural activity with the guidance of other people. The aim is to recognize the essential and inseparable roles of societal heritage, social engagement, and individual efforts. Apprenticeship is guided participation: building bridges between what individuals know and new information or skills to be learned, structuring and supporting the individual's efforts, and transferring to the individual the responsibility for managing problem solving. The suggestions at the end of Chapter Four that focus on developing reflective judgment are grounded in the assumptions of apprenticeship.

Rogoff (1990) contended that the traditional distinction among cognitive, affective, and social processes becomes blurred when we see thinking as the attempt to determine intelligent means to reach goals. Human goals involve other people and carry feelings with them. She quoted Vygotsky (1978, p. 282) to make her point: "Thought . . . is not born of other thoughts. Thought has its origins in the motivating sphere of consciousness, a sphere that includes our inclinations and needs, our interests and impulses, and our affect and emotion. The affective and volitional tendency stands behind thought. Only here do we find the answer to the final 'why' in the analysis of thinking."

In Perry's (1970) scheme, social factors and interpersonal relationships tend to be most obvious in contributing to the process of transitioning from one position to the next. For example, he noted that the stimulus for students who tended toward dualism to move beyond that position often came about when they were confronted with the pluralism of opinions most evident in the residence halls. The first challenge to basic dualism often came from interactions with peers. In addition, students whose view of the world was predominantly multiplicity as correlate (position 4a) believed that all individuals had a right to their own opinions in areas where no clear-cut answer was evident. Their tendency was to challenge Authority (that is, their professors) in order to provide evidence that substantiated their assertions related to areas of contested knowledge. It was often this arguing with professors that led these multiplists to realize that their own arguments needed to be justified with evidence—a hallmark of relativistic thinking. In Perry's scheme, therefore, relationships and interactions were vital for the process of development.

Because many of the women in their study used the metaphor of voice, Belenky, Clinchy, Goldberger, and Tarule (1986) adopted that as the metaphor in their work. Unlike the dominant educational metaphor of seeing and vision, the speaking and listening that are implied by *voice* suggested dialogue and interpersonal interaction. Belenky, Clinchy, Goldberger, and Tarule further argued that the development of voice, mind, and self were intricately intertwined. For women in the position of silence, relationships evidencing mutuality, equality, and reciprocity (that is, interpersonal interaction) helped them to move beyond silence. For women at an advanced perspective, a willingness to ask questions and add to discussion in formal educational settings enhanced their cognitive development. Their connected knowing reflected the importance of social relationships and interaction in the process of cognitive development. It also emphasized the importance of connecting theory and learning to personal experiences. Baxter Magolda (1992) and Belenky, Clinchy, Goldberger, and Tarule (1986), focusing on issues of gender and cognitive development, indicated that women value connectedness or social relationships in their learning experiences to a greater extent than do men but that both men and women benefit from connectedness and positive social relationships in the learning process. This gender-related pattern is also consistent with the findings of Springer, Terenzini, Pascarella, and Nora (1995, p. 16), who found that "time spent socializing with friends was more positively related to gains in orientations toward learning for self-understanding for women than for men." Lundeberg and Diemert Moch (1995) discovered that an emphasis on connected knowing through collaborative supplemental instruction (that is, peer-led discussion groups) helped increase the number of women nursing students who completed required science courses successfully—courses that were archetypal examples of separate knowing (Belenky, Clinchy, Goldberger, and Tarule, 1986). The culture that developed in these peer groups was characterized by a shift in power from leaders to students, increased risk taking, and a spirit of cooperation and community. Lundeberg and Diemert Moch (1995) identified the cognitive aspect of the process as including the confirmation of the student's capacity to learn, an ongoing assessment of student knowledge, and connected learning—in other words, connecting to one another and connecting ideas to experience.

Also, it is important to point out that although interpersonal interaction is vital to development, negative interpersonal interactions can slow or stunt cognitive development. Belenky, Clinchy, Goldberger, and Tarule (1986) pointed out the negative influence of some interpersonal relationships. It was external conditions and, especially, domineering individuals that led to the position of silence for some of the women. In fact, most of the women in their study, at varying points in their development, felt silenced by outside influences. This inhibited their ability to develop cognitively.

Baxter Magolda (1992, 1995) incorporated social relationships into her model of cognitive development and, in fact, indicated that one of the principles guiding her work in exploring students' intellectual development was that "ways of knowing and patterns within them are socially constructed" (1992, p. 20). "One of the most powerful messages in the students' stories," she reported, "was that the ability to develop a distinctive voice stems from defining learning as constructing meaning jointly with others" (1992, p. xiv). She referred to this as relational knowing, which is characterized by attachment and connection with others and with what is known.

Not surprisingly, students also find it difficult to separate social processes from learning and cognitive development (Baxter Magolda, 1992; Belenky, Clinchy, Goldberger, and Tarule, 1986; Kuh, Schuh, and Whitt, 1991; Tinto, Russo, and Kadel, 1994). This influence of social interaction and interpersonal relationships on the process of cognitive development provides the individual professional powerful tools with which to enhance the developmental process. The important role of positive, empowering, democratic, caring, challenging, and supportive interpersonal relationships in cognitive development gives student affairs professionals the opportunity to enhance cognitive development in a number of indirect ways. These ways could include guidance or individual instruction in leadership, assertiveness, conflict mediation, group dynamics, communication skills, debating, listening, mentoring, team building, collaborative problem solving, or community development.

Cultural Influences on Cognitive Development

At the macrosocial level of social influence on cognitive development, the impact of the sociohistorical and cultural contexts on cognitive development is addressed. Sociohistorical influences refer to influences of a particular society at a specific point in time. From the sociohistorical perspective, understanding cognitive development involves both the individual and sociocultural activity, such as schooling (Rogoff, 1990). Cultural context includes the patterns of norms, values, beliefs, and traditions in a group that have an influence on forms of thinking and problem solving and methods of meaning making. Both sociohistorical and cultural issues exist in particular communities. Parker Palmer (1983, p. xv) addressed the issue of knowing and community and their connection to our pervasive culture: "Scholars now understand that knowing is a profoundly communal act. . . . In order to know something, we depend on the consensus of the community in which we are rooted—a consensus so deep that we often draw upon it unconsciously." Culture is one of the subconscious influences on members of a group or society.

One of the most important and pervasive cultural influences on the forms and pace of cognitive development is the system of schooling. Freire (1970) was among the first to point out the influence of cultural assumptions on the lack of cognitive, intellectual, and personal development. He described the "banking method" of education in his native Brazil as one of the accomplices to the totalitarian regime ruling his country at the time. Children were taught (and they internalized) the beliefs that there was only one set of right answers, that they were incapable of knowing, and that they were empty vessels to be filled by learned authorities who possessed all useful knowledge. Others (such as Giroux, 1983, 1988; McLaren, 1989; Shor, 1992) argued persuasively that banking methods of education, though perhaps more subtle than those identified by Freire, pervade American school systems. Pedagogical methods, teacher-student relationships, and the culture of school systems and higher education all shape the forms of cognition, cognitive development, and sense making of students. Therefore, as we change the culture, teacher-student relationships, and methods, we can expect the form and pace of cognitive development to change. Perhaps this evolution is part of what Perry (1981) witnessed when he realized that students finishing their freshman year in the late 1960s were more cognitively advanced than the students of the late 1950s.

As indicated in the section on microsocial influences, Rogoff (1990) argued that cognitive development is an apprenticeship experience that occurs within a sociohistorical context. According to Vygotsky (1978), cognitive skills and patterns of thinking are not determined primarily by innate factors but are the product of activities practiced in the social institutions of the culture (such as family or school) at the time in which the individual grows up (such as the Depression, the 1950s, or the 1990s). In his words: "The tasks with which a society confronts an adolescent as he enters the cultural, professional, and civic world of adults undoubtedly become an important factor in the emergence of conceptual thinking. If the milieu presents no such tasks to the adolescent, makes no new demands on him, and does not stimulate his thinking by providing a sequence of new goals, this thinking fails to reach the highest stages, or reaches them with great delay" (p. 108).

According to this argument, interpersonal interactions can only be understood in the context of the cultural and historical forms in which they take place; the microsocial is intimately connected with the macrosocial. That is, to understand the nature of interaction between students and faculty in a university, reference must be made to the meaning imparted by that particular historically and culturally organized context. For example, Belenky, Clinchy, Goldberger, and Tarule (1986) pointed out that intuition is disregarded in our society. Women who make sense of the world from a subjectivist perspective and utilize intuition as a form of knowing often are dismissed as irrational or illogical in American higher education. Yet in other societies, such as many Asian cultures, intuition is an important element of knowing. Therefore, the relevance of intuition to knowing is an example of how cultural influences affect cognitive development or the perception of the level of cognitive development.

There is also subcultural influence. For example, it is no surprise that what Belenky, Clinchy, Goldberger, and Tarule (1986) found went beyond, and was in some ways different from, what Perry (1970) found. Perry studied a small subgroup of the greater American culture (that is, traditional-aged, white, male, upper class or rich, and overwhelmingly Christian) whereas Belenky, Clinchy, Goldberger, and Tarule, while focusing solely on women, looked at a greater cross section of American culture. In fact, subsequent research has shown that cultural and other social differences affect social interactions within the classroom and, therefore, academic outcomes (Li, 1992; Flores, Cousin, and Diaz, 1991).

Perry conducted much of his research during the 1960s, a decade of tumult and turmoil. The social upheaval of that decade may have had the effect of encouraging a more rapid challenge to authority on the part of college students than had been experienced in the prior decade. It is, therefore, important to consider the societal and cultural influences that may be affecting the cognitive development of college students as we enter the new millennium. First of all, students increasingly are underprepared (Levine and Cureton, 1998). They need remedial help in order to succeed in college. Seventy-three percent of college deans report an increase in the proportion of students requiring remedial or developmental education in the last ten years (Levine and Cureton, 1998). Today nearly one-third of all undergraduates report taking a basic skills or remedial course in reading, writing, or math. The number of students requiring remedial help is expected to increase as we enter the new millennium.

Another stunning change between the adolescents of today and those of the 1950s is their aloneness (Hersch, 1998). The adolescents of the 1990s are more isolated and more unsupervised than other generations. They may lack the necessary apprenticeship experiences to appropriately enhance their cognitive development. For many adolescents today, both parents are at work. Neighbors often are strangers. Relatives live in distant places. Younger and younger children have increasingly greater responsibility for making decisions in their lives. These decisions often are made in a void. Hersch (1998), in a study of adolescents, echoed Rogoff's assertions (1990) related to cognitive development being an apprenticeship experience. Hersch pointed out that since the beginning of time, adolescents have learned to make sense of the world by observing, imitating, and interacting with grown-ups around them. She found it startling how little time modern teenagers spend in the company of adults. In fact, she reported that adolescents spend less than 5 percent of their time with their parents and only 2 percent with other adults. Adult guidance, role modeling, and wisdom are less available to new generations. Their absence will have an impact on how adolescents create meaning and will potentially stunt their cognitive development. An argument can perhaps be made that this situation of premature independence could actually *increase* the rate of cognitive development, in that it forces young people to become better problem solvers. However, as Sanford (1962) pointed out, development occurs where there is a balance of challenge and support. Many of today's adolescents are experiencing extreme challenges without adequate support.

The awareness of societal, cultural, and historical influences on cognitive development should provide insight for professionals seeking to enhance the development of their students. Not surprisingly, professionals need to take into account not only a student's developmental level but also the contexts in which that development did or did not take place. Unfortunately, as Hofer and Pintrich (1997) pointed out, no studies have looked specifically at the cultural nature of cognitive development. Hofer and Pintrich call for more cross-cultural research to determine the influence of Western culture and schooling on cognitive development. Until this research is done, the knowledge and awareness of societal, cultural, and historical influences on cognitive development are not adequate to provide ready means to enhance the cognitive development of college students.

Emotional Influences on Cognitive Development

Issues related to affect and emotion were among the first elements to be carved away from a holistic view of human beings and their development. These internal states of affect and emotion were essentially invisible to the eye and, therefore, perceived as unknowable. Eliminating the recognition of the role of emotion in cognitive development had an inevitable impact on the learning process. In an eight-year study of American schools, Goodlad (1984) found, among other problems, a disturbing lack of positive emotions in the classroom. Given that emotions were "first out" of a holistic view of development, perhaps it is not surprising that they were "last in." In the 1960s, as researchers began to focus on the internal processes of cognition (how the mind registered and stored information), behaviorism (the school of psychology focused only on observable behaviors) waned. At the same time, however, emotions were still off-limits (Goleman, 1995). Only in the last several decades has the influence of emotion on learning and development been integrated with work on cognition and social processes. This integration came after many unsuccessful years of trying to study emotions through physiological measurement. Hastorf and Isen (1982, p. 5) highlighted the difficulty of dealing with affect and cognitive development: "The question of affect . . . has not received much attention in traditional cognitive psychology. . . . Affect is treated as a thing apart, a separate force, a 'spoiler,' to otherwise lawful cognitive relationships. . . . It has promoted corollary views that usually cognition is *unaffected* by affect and motivation, that only strong (and perhaps negative) emotions influence cognition, and that somehow this influence is to interfere with a more basic and otherwise orderly process."

When feeling states and thinking states were separated, research moved away from segregating affect or attempting to physically measure emotions. Instead, researchers concentrated on studying the connection between cognition and the perceptions of feelings. "Cognitive processes themselves," as Hastorf and Isen (1982, p. 6) explained, "are presumed to be complexly constructed and dependent on affective, motivational/contextual, and concurrent cognitive factors." Goleman (1995, pp. 9, 28) described the interrelatedness of feelings and intellect:

> These two minds, the emotional and the rational, operate in tight harmony for the most part, intertwining their very different ways of knowing to guide us through the world. Ordinarily there is a balance between emotional and rational minds, with emotion feeding into and informing the operation of the rational mind, and the rational mind refining and sometimes vetoing the inputs of the emotions. . . . In many or most moments these minds are exquisitely coordinated; feelings are essential to thought, thought to feeling. . . . Feelings are indispensable for rational decisions; they point us in the proper direction, where dry logic can then be of best use.

When studying cognitive development and learning, it is difficult to separate out the role affect plays because learning and cognitive development are facilitated or hampered by emotions, moods, and feelings (Boekaerts, 1993). Piaget viewed emotions "as the energetic source on which the functioning of intelligence depends . . . [and] insisted on a constant interaction and dialectic between affectivity and intelligence" (DeVries and Kohlberg, 1987, p. 33). Sylvester (1994) pointed out that emotion is important in education because it drives attention, which in turn drives learning and memory. Memories formed during a specific emotional state tend to be recalled easily during a subsequent similar emotional state (Thayer, 1989). Sylvester (1994, p. 63) observed, "Classroom simulations and role-playing activities enhance learning because they tie memories to the kinds of emotional contexts in which they will later be used." This type of learning activity may be less useful for traditional testing in that the emotional context of a written exam differs from that of simulations and role plays. These activities may be more beneficial for real-life situations beyond the classroom in which the students will find themselves.

Emotions also affect motivation to learn. Depressed mood states often correlate with decreased motivation in the classroom (Peterson and Seligman, 1984). According to Goleman (1995, p. 78), "Students who are anxious, angry, or depressed don't learn; people who are caught in these states do not take in information efficiently or deal with it well." Bless, Bohner, Schwarz, and Stack (1990) found that individuals in a good mood are more likely to be persuaded in a learning or decision-making situation than those in a bad mood. However, their findings also suggested that the likelihood of effortful, analytical processing of information might decrease as mood states become more positive. That is, the better and happier people feel, the less likely it is that they will subject incoming information to critical analysis, and they may accept it at face value. The complex nature of these findings— that a good mood is beneficial to learning but that perhaps it should not be *too* good—has significant implications for individuals trying to facilitate student learning and cognitive development.

A student's development can be enhanced by actively bringing the dimensions of affect and cognition together. Albert Ellis, the originator of rational-emotive therapy, "believes that affect, behavior, and cognition interact with one another in intricate ways; however, he accords cognition a particularly influential position in these interactions and considers it a more convenient point of intervention than the other processes" (Barrow, 1986, p. 15). Therefore, the intellectual work that goes on in college is an ideal avenue for assisting with students' affective development. Chickering and Reisser (1993, p. 61) concurred: "Assignments that invite students to engage emotionally as well as intellectually can assist them with the management of emotions, which must first be brought into awareness before they can be given powerful expression." Page and Page (1993) discovered that goal setting and problem solving developed students' self-esteem by enhancing their perception of competence—another link between cognitive processes and affective development.

Research also has been conducted on the interrelationship of emotional skills and aptitudes on college outcomes. Goleman (1995) reported on several studies where emotional skills were better predictors of various measures of academic success than was IQ. For example, one study of four-year-olds showed in a simple experiment involving marshmallows that those who were unable to delay gratification and control impulses had significantly lower SAT scores fourteen years later than those who could wait for gratification. In the experiment each child received one marshmallow; if she could wait fifteen minutes before eating it, then she got two marshmallows. The SATs showed a 210-point difference between the average score for those who could not wait (1052) and the average score for those who could (1262). In another study (Goleman, 1995) a student's level of hope, defined as "believing you have both the will and the way to accomplish your goals" (p. 86), was a better predictor of first-semester grades than were SAT scores. Still another study (Goleman, 1995) discovered that first-year students' scores on a test of optimism, described as "the strong expectation that, in general, things will turn out all right in life despite setbacks and frustrations" (p. 88), were better predictors of grades for the first year than were their SAT scores or their high school grades. Goleman (1995) concluded that given about the same range of intellectual abilities and emotional skills, the ability to delay gratification, have hope, and be optimistic makes the critical difference. The good news is that despite the claims that training cannot raise IQ scores, an improvement in emotional abilities can. Emotional abilities can enhance cognitive abilities and development, as well as academic achievement.

Research also supports the theory that an emotionally positive classroom climate facilitates learning and enhances students' academic achievement and cognitive development (Li, 1992; Seiler, 1989). Connell (1990) found that students in classrooms where they have a sense of belonging or "relatedness"—places where affect and interpersonal interactions intersect— yielded higher scores on measures of perceived academic control. Students who felt emotionally secure with classmates and faculty were more likely to be active participants in class and to exert more effort in their work, thus maintaining and enhancing their academic achievement (Cabello and Terrell, 1994; Tinto and Goodsell, 1993). For at-risk students (students with lowered aspirations, low self-esteem, low internal locus of control, negative attitudes toward school, history of failure, fractured families, substance abuse problems) the single most frequent perception was that their teachers did not care about them (Kagan, 1990), which in turn would serve to block their cognitive development.

Negative feelings (such as depression, hopelessness, anger, anxiety) hinder one's ability and tendency to develop cognitively. Individual intervention in addressing the root causes of these emotions can serve not only to help relieve the negative emotion and encourage positive emotions but also to remove obstacles to a student's cognitive development. Maslow (1987, pp. 102–103) pointed out that "Every good human being is potentially an unconscious therapist. . . . Every person who is kind, helpful, decent, psychologically democratic, affectionate, and warm is a psychotherapeutic force." His point was that professionals do not need to be trained psychotherapists to help address negative emotional states. Professionals need to be aware of the influence of negative emotions on learning and development and work to address them.

Conclusion

Interpersonal and cultural influences on cognitive development appear to be external factors influencing the process of development. They can either be positive (such as enhancing, motivating, amplifying) or negative (such as inhibiting, diminishing, blocking). Affective states, or emotions, are internal factors that can either enhance cognitive development or inhibit it.

Palmer (1987) asserted that negative emotion detracts from interpersonal connectedness, which in turn precludes an effective focus on learning and cognitive development. He indicated that fear of conflict in teaching and learning leads both students and faculty away from developing communities, thereby reducing interpersonal interactions and reducing the opportunities for intellectual development. On the other hand, positive emotional climates enhance the sense of community and allow that community to work together toward mutual understanding, enhanced learning, and individual development. As Palmer (1987, p. 25) suggested: "What prevents [creative] conflict in our classrooms is a very simple emotion called fear. . . . It's fear of exposure, of appearing ignorant, or being ridiculed. And the only antidote to that fear is a hospitable environment created, for example, by a teacher who knows how to use every remark, no matter how mistaken or seemingly stupid, to upbuild both the individual and the group. . . . Community is precisely that place where an arena for creative conflict is protected by the compassionate fabric of human caring itself." King and Baxter Magolda (1996, pp. 163–164) provided another example that specifies the interrelatedness of cognitive, social, and affective elements of development:

> The qualities associated with a college-educated person include more than the cognitive ability to engage in critical thinking; they also include such affective attributes as an eagerness to continue to learn, an appreciation of the value of working with diverse others on problems of mutual interest, the will to take personal responsibility for one's views and actions, and the desire to make a positive contribution. . . . For example, effective conflict mediation can require not only a complex understanding of the underlying issues (cognitive complexity), but also the ability to open and continue a dialogue between disputing parties (interpersonal skills) and an understanding of the limits of one's role (personal maturity).

It must be noted that negative or dysfunctional elements within any of the four domains (adding cultural to interpersonal, affective, and cognitive) will also negatively influence the other three. However, the interrelatedness of the interpersonal, cultural, emotional, and cognitive elements of cognitive development also provides professionals with multiple avenues through which to understand and address students' cognitive development.

6

Kegan's orders of consciousness are useful in developing a holistic understanding of college students' ways of knowing that incorporates their thinking, feeling, and social relating.

Kegan's Orders of Consciousness

Robert Kegan first introduced his theory of meaning making and the evolution of consciousness in *The Evolving Self: Problem and Process in Human Development* (1982). His subsequent book, *In Over Our Heads: The Mental Demands of Modern Life* (1994), extended his original theory and framed it in the context of the mental demands that the "curriculum" of modern life makes on adults. Here Kegan used the theory as an analytical tool to examine contemporary culture and illustrated his constructs using examples from multiple arenas of life (partnering, parenting, working, dealing with difference, learning).

A psychologist with a background in the humanities, Kegan acknowledged the inspiration of Erik Erikson and particularly Jean Piaget on his own thinking and his constructive-developmental theory. He also worked closely with and learned from both Lawrence Kohlberg and William Perry at Harvard. He classifies his theory as a "neo-Piagetian" approach that focuses on the person as an "ever progressive motion engaged in giving itself a new form" (Kegan, 1982, p. 8). Kegan (1982, p. vii) describes himself as a teacher, therapist, and researcher who seeks to engage others through his work in "an exploration of just how much can be understood about a person by understanding his or her meaning system."

According to Kegan (1982), meaning making is a physical activity (grasping, seeing), a social activity (it requires another), and a survival activity (in doing it, we live). It is an intrinsically cognitive activity, but it is no less affective. His 1982 work describes the individual's personal evolution of meaning as a balancing and rebalancing of subject and object, or self and other. *The Evolving Self* describes six different levels of sense making that occur throughout the life span. The basic premise of *In Over Our Heads* is that there exists a "mismatch" between the culture's complex "curriculum" and our mental capacity to deal with the demands of adult living. If educators purport to prepare students for the demands of life after college, this "mismatch" must concern them and shape the educational agenda for college students.

Although Kegan's work seldom specifically addresses college student development, it is valuable in understanding this development in the wider context of the life span. Moreover, unlike the other cognitive theories examined in this volume, his theory addresses cognitive, social, and emotional development together as elements of a system of meaning formation. Though the language, terminology, and graphic representation Kegan uses to describe the framework of his theory change from his 1982 work to his 1994 work, the underlying theoretical constructs remain the same. The explanation below uses his more recent description and language while attempting to capture the fullness of the theory as described in both sources. In 1982, Kegan described his theory as "empirically grounded speculation" (p. ix) based on his years as a therapist and teacher. The 1994 extension is further grounded in cross-sectional studies and longitudinal research conducted by Kegan and colleagues using the Subject-Object Interview (Lahey and others, 1988), which they developed at Harvard after Kegan's original work was published.

The Subject-Object Distinction

Central to comprehending Kegan's theory is an understanding of the subject-object distinction. In simplest terms, we *are* subject and we *have* object. Subject is that which we cannot see because it comprises us. We therefore cannot be responsible for or in control of it, nor can we reflect on it. The root *ject* in *object* refers to the motion or activity of throwing. *Object* can be understood to refer to that which meaning making has made separate and distinct from us. Kegan (1994, p. 32) offers the following definitions:

> "Subject" refers to those elements of our knowing or organizing that we are identified with, tied to, fused with, or embedded in.
>
> "Object" refers to those elements of our knowing or organizing that we can reflect on, handle, look at, be responsible for, relate to each other, take control of, internalize, assimilate, or otherwise act upon.

An example is a preteen who is able to assert her independence from her parents and advocate forcefully for her needs (newly acquired abilities because her separateness and impulses, which earlier in her life were inseparable from her sense of self, are now *object*). However, she is yet unable to consider the needs and feelings of others in her decision making and actions (because her needs, interests, and wishes are still *subject*).

Kegan's Five Orders of Consciousness

Kegan's theory centers around five "orders of consciousness," which are principles of mental organization that affect thinking, feeling, and relating to self and others. Kegan uses the term *order* to indicate a dimensional quality (that is, a level) rather than a strict sequence (such as the term *stage* suggests). Each successive principle transcends the last in that the new way of knowing incorporates the meaning-making abilities of the last and the individual becomes able to reflect on these abilities. In addition to its cognitive properties, each order has both *intra*personal (self-concept) and *inter*personal (relationship) dimensions.

Two of these orders, the first and fifth, are not directly applicable to the experiences of undergraduate college students. Children make the transition from first- to second-order thinking between the ages of five and ten, long before college. Regarding the other end of the continuum, Kegan (1994, p. 352) indicates that "it is rare to see people moving beyond the fourth order, but when they do, it is never before their forties." Therefore, this summary will touch only briefly on the first and fifth orders.

The potential to affect college students' development intentionally is most powerful in the transitions between orders of consciousness. In fact, Kegan's concept of the person as continually evolving makes directing our attention to the transitions, rather than to the temporary balance represented by each "order," much more theoretically consistent. The following analysis therefore pays particular attention to the two transitional periods student affairs educators are most likely to encounter: from the second to the third order and from the third to the fourth order.

Fundamental Assumptions. Five important assumptions underlie Kegan's theory. First, the orders of consciousness not only refer to how one thinks but more generally to how one constructs experience, which includes thinking, feeling, and relating to others. Second, Kegan's orders concern the *organization* of one's thinking, feeling, and social relating rather than the *content*. Third, each order of consciousness is constituted by a different subject-object relationship. Kegan's fourth assumption is that the orders of consciousness are related to each other. One does not simply replace the other; rather, each successive principle subsumes the prior principle. Thus, the new order is higher, more complex, and more inclusive. Finally, what is taken as subject and object is not fixed: what was subject at one order becomes object at the next order. Therefore, there is a developing ability to relate to or see that in which we were formerly enmeshed. Figure 6.1 summarizes elements of the orders of consciousness and portrays the movement of subject toward becoming object in the next order of consciousness.

First Order of Consciousness. At the first order of consciousness, young children (from birth to age seven or eight) do not have the capacity for abstract thought. Rather, physical objects principally represent the child's momentary

Figure 6.1. Summary of Orders of Consciousness

Order	Subject	Object	Focus	Thinking
First: Single point, immediate	Fantasy, impulse, perception	Movement and sensation	Particulars	Concrete
Second: Durable categories	Self-concept, needs, preferences	Fantasy, impulse, perception	Structures, categories	Relating concrete concepts
Third: Cross-categorical thinking	Abstractions, mutuality, subjectivity	Self-concept, needs, preferences	Abstract thinking, relationships	Abstract
Fourth: Cross-categorical constructing	Ideology, multiple roles, self-authorship	Abstractions, mutuality, subjectivity	Constructing, self-authoring	Relating abstract concepts
Fifth: Transsystem	Oppositeness, interpenetration of self and others, interindividuation	Ideology, multiple roles, self-authorship	Multipleness	Systems

perceptions of them. Meaning is made from a very egocentric, fantasy-filled position. The world is not concrete, and there is no realization that others have separate minds, separate intentions, and separate vantage points.

At this order, children are able to recognize objects separate from self, but those objects are subject to the children's perception of them. Thus, from the children's perspective, if their perception of an object changes, the object itself changes. Children come to *have* reflexes rather than *be* them, and the self is that which coordinates the reflexes through perceptions and impulses. Impulse control is not possible because children are subject to their impulses, and nonexpression raises the threat of risking "who I am."

Second Order of Consciousness. From late childhood until sometime in adolescence or early adulthood, individuals make meaning by learning to construct "durable categories"—lasting classifications in which physical objects, people, and desires come to have properties of their own that characterize them as distinct from "me." In the transition from first- to second-order consciousness, momentary impulses and immediate perceptions move from being the subject to being the object of experiencing. The new subject becomes the durable category.

In the construction of durable categories, physical objects, people, and desires change from being seen solely from the individual's momentary perceptions of them. The ability develops to classify them according to their properties using ongoing rules that are not dependent on individual perceptions. For example, a child comes to recognize that some animals fall into the category "dog" whereas others do not fit into this category because of properties such as fins, trunks, or wings. Children now recognize that they are individuals with characteristics, and this creates a self-concept. In addition, other people become "property-bearing selves distinct from me" (Kegan, 1994, p. 23). For example, distinctions between family, friends, and strangers become possible: some are friendly and fun; others are uncomfortable and stiff when they are around kids.

Desires change from being principally about moment-to-moment impulses or wishes to being about ongoing needs or preferences. For instance, individuals begin to classify themselves as people who like to read, enjoy playing sports, or hate vegetables. A shift from a fantasy orientation to a reality orientation occurs in which individuals begin to develop self-sufficiency and take on the social role of a child. A capacity develops to "take the role" of another and to see that others have a perspective of their own.

Individuals are still concerned primarily with the pursuit and satisfaction of their own interests, are not yet able to own membership in a wider community than the one defined by self-interest, and are not yet able to think abstractly. At the second order, individuals' actions are determined in the context of their own point of view or needs. However, a primary determinant of how they feel is how others will react to their actions.

Transition from the Second to the Third Order. Between ages twelve and twenty, the gradual transformation of mind from the second to the third order takes place. Though likely to occur during adolescence, this transition may also take place as young adults enter college or, less likely, during the collegiate experience. Society's mental demands most likely have already resulted in this transition for adult learners.

Kegan notes that many adolescents are unable to meet the expectations the adult culture holds of them. Thus, student affairs educators should consider whether the expectations held of beginning college students are appropriate for their developmental level. If thinking abstractly and seeing oneself as a member of a community are required, students in the midst of this transition may need some real support and guidance as they develop this type of thinking.

If individuals do not yet construct the particular way of knowing demanded of them, "the difficulty might be more a matter of not understanding the rules of the game than one of an unwillingness to play" (Kegan, 1994, p. 38). Student affairs professionals must help students understand the "rules of the game" (such as behavioral expectations and responsibilities) so that they are able to meet the expectations society and college have of them. For example, if the expectation is that students be able to take other people's feelings into account even when considering themselves, this might be insisting on "rules of a game" that students still at the second order of consciousness are not yet able to comprehend.

Those working with students can help them see how their point of view relates to that of others or accept when their particular preferences or needs must be subordinated to those of others. These issues arise in the familiar conflicts between roommates in residence halls (for example, when one student is unable to understand how the constant presence of her boyfriend in the room infringes on her roommate's privacy) or when individual rights must be limited to accommodate the best interests of a larger whole (such as when a student living in a residence hall is asked to turn down his stereo in consideration of others' need to study). Opportunities to learn about themselves in a reflective manner when values, broad beliefs, and social roles are considered can assist students in making this transition.

Third Order of Consciousness. In this order of consciousness, one is able to "think abstractly, identify a complex internal psychological life, orient to the welfare of a human relationship, construct values and ideals self-consciously . . . and subordinate one's own interests" (Kegan, 1994, p. 75). The primary capacity of this order is the ability to experience the self in relation to a given category rather than as the category itself. For example, individuals might start to reflect on the *type* of friends they are. Individuals also begin to consider not just what will happen to them or to their wants but what will happen to the bonds or relationships in their life. As a result, individuals become able to subordinate some of their own interests to a shared interest instead of only being able to get their own needs met.

At this order, in addition to the ability to construct one's own point of view, the recognition emerges that others are constructing their own point of view as well. Individuals can further subordinate their own point of view to the relationship between their point of view and that of others. This requires movement from "I am my point of view" to "I have a point of view." Prosocial expectations, such as being a good citizen, require this type of cross-categorical knowing. For example, a college student may start to consider the effect a choice to stay out all night may have on the roommate who worries that something may have happened and to consider how that might affect their relationship.

Cross-categorical thinking also makes possible experiencing emotions as inner psychological states. This requires integrating the simpler, categorical self into a more complex context that *relates to* the self. For example, rather than simply experiencing depression (emotion as subject—I am depressed), individuals might recognize themselves as being in a state of depression as opposed to a normal state of being (emotion as object—I am experiencing depression). It is also at the third order of consciousness that values, ideals, and broad beliefs can be constructed. The previous, more concrete way of thinking allowed individuals only to consider themselves as honest or dishonest people rather than as people who value honesty and strive to live up to that ideal (whether or not it is always attained).

Transition from the Third to the Fourth Order. Kegan asserts that this is the principal transformation of consciousness in adulthood. It basically involves attaining self-authorship: the ability to "write" one's own life. Educational settings can provide a conducive context for it to occur. At the third order of consciousness, the system by which individuals make meaning still rests outside the self, in realities shared with others. Kegan speaks of this as being both "the triumph and limit of the third order" (Kegan, 1994, p. 126). In gaining the ability to become part of a community or society, individuals triumph. However, they are still limited by being unable to stand apart from this co-construction to reflect and act on it.

The transition to the fourth order is sometimes signaled when a student feels life has suddenly come to a halt or when a student loses concentration, energy, and purpose. Students may describe themselves as having become lazy or even angry as they struggle to extricate self from others' expectations (which have become excessive or seem to conflict) and to determine "Who is in charge around here, anyway?" The precipitating event for this shift can be the loss of an important relationship, whether self-initiated or through rejection or betrayal, because at the third order, students *are* their relationships (subject) rather than *having* them (object).

Students begin to develop an independent selfhood with an ideology of their own and will often insist on being taken seriously as an adult and equal. The source of judgment and expectation comes to reside within the self rather than being confused with others. For example, guilt might be experienced as a result of a violation of one's own internal standard, irrespective of others' expectations. Going away to college "can provide a new evolutionary medium that recognizes and cultures the moves toward self-authorship" (Kegan, 1982, p. 186).

Being caught between one way of meaning making and another can be very disruptive and painful. This is particularly true in the transition of the structure of "relationship" from subject to object, during which students may experience loss and loneliness, as well as a feeling of selfishness. Educators can offer students several types of support in this transition: recognition of students as independent individuals in their own right; an opportunity for publicly recognized personal achievement; a chance to participate in a group based on an aspect of their self-authored identity; and guidance regarding entry into the world of work.

Fourth Order of Consciousness. Kegan labels the fourth order of consciousness "cross-categorical constructing" (as opposed to third-order "cross-categorical thinking"), highlighting the individual's new ability to construct generalizations across abstractions. An internally consistent organization (identity) comes into being that uses a formal system to relate concrete and context-bound particulars, as well as abstractions. However, "one-half to two-thirds of the adult population appear not to have fully reached the fourth order of consciousness" (Kegan, 1994, p. 191).

This order represents a step beyond the third-order capacity to generalize across concrete particulars and form cross-categorical structures, such as values. Individuals who reach this order develop the capacity to stand outside of their values and form a deeper internal set of convictions that form a context for and regulate behavior. These values *about* values provide a means for choosing among values when they conflict. Rather than being regulated by and held to the standard of a value, ideal, or belief, an individual at the fourth order would have to be able to "subordinate a perfectly respectable ideal (like 'openness and honesty') to a bigger theory or ideology that can regulate the ideal" (Kegan, 1994, pp. 89–90). An example is when a student weighs a larger principle, such as "doing no harm," against how much honesty is called for when she suspects her best friend's partner of being unfaithful.

The making of an ideology involves an ability "to subordinate, regulate, and indeed create (rather than be created by) our values and ideals—the ability to take values and ideals as the object rather than the subject of our knowing" (Kegan, 1994, p. 91). This capacity is referred to as *self-authorship* and incorporates the ideas of self-regulation, identity, autonomy, and individuation, as opposed to relying on others to frame the problems or determine whether things are going acceptably well.

The capacity for self-authorship is a qualitatively more complex system for organizing experience than the mental operations of previous orders, which create values, beliefs, generalizations, abstractions, interpersonal loyalty, and intrapersonal states of mind. It is an internal identity that can coordinate, integrate, or act on them. It also fosters a sense of identity that is "more enduring than earlier co-constructed versions because the internal self is the source of belief rather than the social surround that was the source of the belief in the third order" (Baxter Magolda, forthcoming, pp. 2–3).

Interpersonally, this ability translates into the capacity to stand outside a relationship and make judgments about its demands without feeling the relationship itself has thereby been fundamentally violated. An "I" is brought into being that *has,* rather than *is,* its relationships. In moving beyond another's expectations or claims, an individual utilizing fourth-order consciousness can create a larger mental context that involves a "relationship to the relationship" (Kegan, 1994, p. 92). An example is when individuals realize they have become too dependent on a relationship with a partner as the source of their personal happiness. Realizing this dependence, one can look at ways to become less reliant on the relationship as a source of satisfaction and fulfillment, without changing or ending the relationship itself.

Self-authorship is an outcome reflected in many universities' mission statements and a goal for many divisions of student affairs: to foster the student's development as a self-directed learner, an individual who acts on the world for the betterment of society (rather than is acted on), and an engaged citizen with a strong sense of values and a clear identity that is internally defined. Kegan argues persuasively that in order to be effective as partners, as parents, in work, and in leading, individuals must be capable of self-authorship.

Fifth Order of Consciousness. Fifth-order thinking is relatively rare and never appears before individuals reach their forties (Kegan, 1994). An individual's identity system moves from subject to object and brings into being a new interindividual way of organizing reality that emphasizes a refusal to see oneself or the other as a single system or form. This order is built on a realization of the human tendency to pretend toward completeness while actually being incomplete. It is only in relationship that we are who we are.

This is a "somewhat controversial" claim as it "flies in the face of cherished notions of maturity" (Kegan, 1982, p. 228) by suggesting that a highly differentiated psychological autonomy may not be the fullest picture of maturity. Rather, it suggests a notion of development beyond the autonomy of establishing one's identity and points to a level of development that relies on the individual being able to experience a sharing or intimacy with others.

At this order individuals begin to use a perspective of "multipleness." Relationships become "a context for a sharing and an interacting . . . in which the *many* forms or systems that *each self is* are helped to emerge" (Kegan, 1994, p. 313). Individuals hold suspect their sense of their own and each other's wholeness; they reject false assumptions of distinctness or completeness. The self-as-system is seen as incomplete—only a partial construction of all that the self is. It is the process of creating self through relationships that is imperative.

The shift to this way of meaning making can be accompanied by an experience of losing one's balance or a sense that one's personal organization is threatened or about to collapse. A sense of boundaries being violated may be felt. Fears also may develop about losing one's control and sense of being distinct.

One of the central features of this new way of thinking is an orientation toward contradiction and paradox. Rather than feeling a need to choose between the two poles in a paradox, an individual recognizes the contradiction and orients toward the relationship between the poles. Therefore, contradictions do not threaten the system or necessarily need to be reconciled.

In an attempt to illustrate and clarify this complex concept, Kegan gives the example of a cylinder, which can be seen as a glass tube that has two openings. On the other hand, using a fifth-order perspective, "we could conclude that what the cylinder really is, is two openings connected by a glass tube. We could see the glass tube as the connector or relater of the two ends" (Kegan, 1994, p. 313). This is the view of relationships from the fifth order, which focuses on the bond or link between the parts. For example, individuals at the fifth order of consciousness might view their own leadership style as providing a context in which all constituencies involved, the leader included, can together create a vision, mission, or purpose that can collectively be upheld.

Creating Bridges to More Complex Orders

Kegan's focus has been to develop and illustrate his theory within the general context of the demands of adult life. Therefore, a degree of translation and extension is necessary to obtain specific implications for working with college students outside the classroom. Key concepts and strategies with substantial promise for applicability to student affairs practice include coaching, holding environments, and bridge building.

Student affairs practitioners need to be effective in creating environments where challenge and support are blended to foster students' growth. Kegan asserts that society in general is far better at providing challenges than supporting individuals' growth. The college environment also may be providing more than adequate challenge. Nonetheless, as Kegan (1994) maintains, it is not necessarily a bad thing to be "in over our heads," provided there is effective support available. Today's college students are living in a time of profound change and facing enormous pressure—economically, politically, socially, and psychologically (Levine and Cureton, 1998). Perhaps in the challenging environment of today's college campus, students' overwhelming need is for support.

Kegan suggests the concept of "sympathetic coaching" to provide the needed support. Sympathetic coaches have a concern for the developmental process within a successful program or popular activity. They provide "welcoming acknowledgment to exactly who the person is right now as he or she is" (Kegan, 1994, p. 43) while an individual is gradually outgrowing a way of knowing the world.

Confirmation for the students' current way of meaning making is not the only function of sympathetic coaches; they must also "nurture the seeds of its productive undoing" (Kegan, 1994, p. 45) by providing contradiction that supports the *transformation* of knowing. Student affairs professionals must recognize and respect where the students are, thus gaining their interest and involvement in the intervention, yet provide glimpses of and attractive opportunities to try out aspects of the next higher order. For example, students using the second order of consciousness might initially be enticed to participate in community service by emphasizing opportunities for increased personal competence and personal reward. Once individuals are "hooked," they may begin to change their way of meaning making with regard to the service activities. They may start to recognize that in order to gain their desired outcomes, they need to become members in a community of interest greater than themselves and to subordinate their own welfare to that of others. Eventually they may even feel a loyalty to or identification with the individuals being served. Engaging others in service by appealing to personal gains and rewards may be a technique professionals use in facilitating community service programming. Yet, how many truly acknowledge or welcome the students who approach in this manner? And how often is this seen as an opportunity to promote development of consciousness?

Kegan identifies two primary ways that educators fail to provide support: by neglecting to build a bridge out of and beyond the old world and by expecting individuals to take up immediate residence in the new world. Although educators should never be critical of where students are, they must do more than acknowledge and support students where they are. Kegan suggests that educators should "fashion a bridge that is more respectfully anchored on both sides of the chasm, instead of assuming that such a bridge already exists and wondering why the other has not long ago walked over it" (Kegan, 1994, p. 332).

Kegan's theory addresses the environment of development more explicitly than any of the other cognitive theories examined in this volume. He asserts that sympathetic coaches can be developmentally supportive through their role as part of the psychosocial environment in which individuals develop. The term *holding environment* specifically recognizes one of the primary functions of the environment—its function to hold securely by confirming and supporting as opposed to keeping or confining.

Peers are also important elements of holding environments, being part of the old way of knowing and also part of the new. For example, relationships with peers can facilitate movement from the second to the third order of consciousness by providing an opportunity to "get inside" a view separate from one's own. Even if the other's point of view is perceived as being basically the same as one's own, slight differences inevitably emerge. As individuals try to restore a sense of their identity between the two views, a completely different order of consciousness can emerge. Peer relationships also provide opportunities for transition to the fourth order as individuals begin to consider their relationship to these relationships.

Kegan's theory underscores the value of creating programs that are highly acknowledging of, and sensible to, students' current ways of meaning making while at the same time promoting the development of the next higher order of consciousness. The programs must artfully recognize and welcome the individual's current order of consciousness while "quite deliberately creat[ing] the circumstances for its productive undoing" (Kegan, 1994, p. 46). This can be done by placing values consistent with the higher order *not* in the foreground but in the background of the program and by communicating with participants at the most fundamental level of their meaning making. For instance, a program that insists that participants work in groups, learn each other's skills and limitations as well as their own, and hold each other in mind even as they pursue their own ends facilitates third-order thinking. However, the key to interesting and engaging the students in the program (the "hook") must be aimed at their current level of meaning formation.

It is most important for educators to realize that if their interest is actually to engage, or in some way relate to, their students, they must first understand their students. Educators must hold themselves "to the rigors of addressing the person in the experience of meaning-making, rather than the meaning the person has made" (Kegan, 1994, p. 293). Baxter Magolda (forthcoming) illustrates this primary tenet of Kegan's theory in her suggestion that focusing on how the third order of mind makes meaning might lead to better understanding of common campus issues, such as abusive dating relationships, alcohol abuse, or hazing. Kegan's theory provides a powerful lens though which to view and learn about college students and support them in their developmental evolution.

7

This chapter melds the research and theories, provides a tool with which to informally assess the cognitive development of college students, and presents information on how to apply these theories in practice.

Synthesis, Assessment, and Application

In the previous chapters of this book, we have presented theories and research related to the cognitive development of college students as well as an examination of the interpersonal, cultural, and emotional influences on cognitive development. Each chapter has presented a single theory of cognitive development with its own definitions, conceptual framework, and methodology for examining ways of thinking and knowing. The purpose of this chapter is threefold: to offer a basic synthesis and comparison of that varied work; to describe a method for informally assessing the cognitive development of students; and to provide ideas as to how to apply cognitive development theory in student affairs practice.

In synthesizing the five major theories presented previously in this volume, we address the points of intersection and commonalities but also indicate where the theories and research diverge. We find similarities among the models as well as distinct emphases and differences. We believe we can gain insight from overlaying the models and increase our understanding of college students' cognitive development by studying them collectively. We first synthesize the four theories related to Perry's scheme, then follow with a comparison to Kegan's work. In addition, we address the issues of gender and culture in cognitive development. Next, we discuss methods of intentional informal assessment of students' cognitive development. Finally, we explore the practical educational applications of the theories of cognitive development reviewed in this volume.

Points of Intersection and Divergence

It seems that however many positions, stages, or levels each of the theorists may propose, each theory contains three main categories of epistemological views. Kuhn's (1991) work in argumentative reasoning and epistemological perspectives similarly identifies three basic categories: absolutist, multiplist, and evaluative. Though the classification presented here parallels Kuhn's work in many respects, we have chosen to define the three primary perspectives on knowing as unequivocal knowing, radical subjectivity, and generative knowing. Unequivocal knowers experience the world as ultimately known (or knowable) and knowledge and truth as universal, certain, and dispensed by authorities. Radical subjectivists begin to recognize uncertainty, which causes them to leave the certainty of unequivocal knowing without having developed the full capacity to deal effectively with this transition. Without a means of determining what can be known, opinion becomes authority and even the authority of experts, which was heretofore recognized, is diminished. In order for the powerful transition to the next category to occur, the "great accommodation" must take place. At this point the knower rejects the notion that all views have equal legitimacy and develops a way to deal with the uncertainty of knowledge. Generative knowers are individuals experiencing ongoing development in a world accepted as ambiguous, incompletely knowable, and complex. They understand knowledge as contextual and accept their central role in constructing it.

Unequivocal Knowing. Each of the theories reviewed in this book describes an early perspective in which knowers view the world as having a single, universal truth—a truth that is known to authorities who have the ability to pass that knowledge on to others. Truth and knowledge are external to the knower. Whatever knowers themselves may "know" is neither truth nor knowledge. What is "known" might be labeled as experience or opinion, but these types of "knowledge" are species different from truth and knowledge. Knowledge is possessed by authorities, often persons such as parents, teachers, priests, ministers, or rabbis. Authority also may exist in artifacts, such as the Constitution, the Bible, or other published materials. Knowledge and truth are not open to questioning. They are universal and context free, meaning that they are everywhere the same and do not change over time.

Whatever a particular theorist may call this stage or position (such as dualism, received knowledge, absolute knowing, pre-reflective thinking), it appears that a pure version is not likely to be found among college students. Although there may be knowledge domains in students' experience where there is a nearly pure form of this position (such as religious beliefs), most would not experience this type of sense making generalized across all knowledge domains. In fact, we would argue on the basis of these theoretical perspectives that in order for a college student to maintain this type of thinking, it would have to either be imposed from the outside (that is, through social or environmental influence, such as in the perspective of silence identified by Belenky, Clinchy, Goldberger, and Tarule, 1986) or be the result of some emotional disorder or psychopathology. However, we do acknowledge that some individuals may retreat from situations of overwhelming complexity in a temporary adaptation that may resemble the naive condition of this initial way of meaning making.

Radical Subjectivism. Each of the theories also describes the gradual breakdown in the view of knowledge, truth, and authority as absolute through a process where uncertainty, ambiguity, and complexity creep into and disturb the sense-making process. This uncertainty and ambiguity may initially be resisted, viewed as temporary, or written off as anomalous. The student experiences a sense of confusion, as if being suddenly thrust into a game without any clear rules to determine right and wrong. Eventually, the individual reaches a sort of détente with uncertainty—it exists and must be tolerated. However, for lack of any way to mediate among alternative explanations or rationales, the student adopts the position that all views are equally valid and that opinions are sources of truth. Some may assert a "right" to their own opinion; others see truth as an intuitive and personally experienced reaction.

The Great Accommodation. Among the many accommodations experienced by students as they develop cognitively, the greatest of these appears to be the accommodation of moving from viewing the world as predominantly known, certain, and knowable to viewing the world as predominantly ambiguous, complex, and not completely knowable. The great accommodation occurs when the individual comes to realize that uncertainty is neither anomalous nor restricted to certain knowledge domains—that it is evident everywhere. As the place of knowledge, truth, and authority disintegrates, the individual's own role as knower and authority emerges. Perry (1970, p. 121) refers to a transformation in worldview that he terms a "revolutionary restructuring." The accommodation is complete when uncertainty, ambiguity, and complexity are accepted as the norm and one's experience and opinion are considered in light of the knowledge and truths of experts and authorities.

Generative Knowing. Beyond the "great accommodation," the theories diverge somewhat, exploring and explaining subtly different forms of knowing and sense making as each defines the construct at its most complex level in a slightly different manner. Perry (1970) emphasizes the relative nature of knowledge; that is, knowledge is related to other knowledge, contexts, and experience. Beyond relativism, he ventures into ethical and identity development to tentatively explore the role of commitments in relativism, but he leaves this part of his theory underdeveloped. King and Kitchener (1994) go on to elaborate structural and epistemological aspects beyond relativism, focusing on the use of critical inquiry and probabilistic justification to guide knowledge construction. Belenky, Clinchy, Goldberger, and Tarule (1986) describe an integration of subjective and objective strategies for knowing. Baxter Magolda (1992) focuses on the merging of the gender-related reasoning patterns evidenced in her earlier ways of knowing to produce a knower capable of constructing an individual perspective by judging evidence in context.

What all of the theories have in common at this point is a conception of the knower coming into a sense of agency in the knowing process. Students realize their active role in considering context, comparing and evaluating viewpoints to assess relative merits, and constructing an individual perspective on issues. Therefore, generative knowers have the power to generate, produce, originate, or author their own truths. In addition, at this level students evidence the capability of metacognition—a capacity to think about thought. Though each theory varies considerably in methodologies used to examine epistemological beliefs and thinking, all four indicate that generative knowing would be rare at the undergraduate level but more common among graduate students. In general, undergraduate college students are approaching or struggling with the "great accommodation," the successful management of which would allow them to reach this level of knowing.

Further Comparison and Kegan's Theory

We argue that these theories taken together are stronger than any single theory on its own. First, two of the theories (Perry's and Baxter Magolda's) focus primarily on the development of college students whereas the others (Belenky, Clinchy, Goldberger, and Tarule's, King and Kitchener's, and Kegan's) situate development during college within the life span by studying adults of various ages from both within and outside higher education settings. Second, Perry's work and Belenky, Clinchy, Goldberger, and Tarule's theory are based on cross-sectional studies; Baxter Magolda's work is longitudinal in design; and the studies on which King and Kitchener's theory and Kegan's framework are based include both cross-sectional and longitudinal studies. Third, the theories are built on forms of inquiry that, taken together, complement each other well. Perry, Baxter Magolda, and Belenky, Clinchy, Goldberger, and Tarule used a phenomenological approach in the qualitative research tradition; King and Kitchener and Kegan used a more quantitative approach with structured interviewing techniques. Fourth, gender issues are addressed more fully through a composite view. As Hofer and Pintrich (1997) point out, Perry's work is a pioneering study of men only; Belenky, Clinchy, Goldberger, and Tarule provide a comparable study of women; and Baxter Magolda describes gender-related patterns in a study that includes both men and women. King and Kitchener's theory is also built on male and female participants though the results concerning gender differences in development are inconclusive. Accounting for the complexity of the theories that have been reviewed is impossible in this volume. However, Figure 7.1 shows a comparison of the theories. This figure directly contrasts the component stages, positions, and perspectives of the five theories. Although included in this comparison, Kegan's orders of consciousness differ from the other four theories in several important ways. Kegan's theory incorporates interpersonal and affective sense making directly. It also

Figure 7.1. Comparison of the Theories

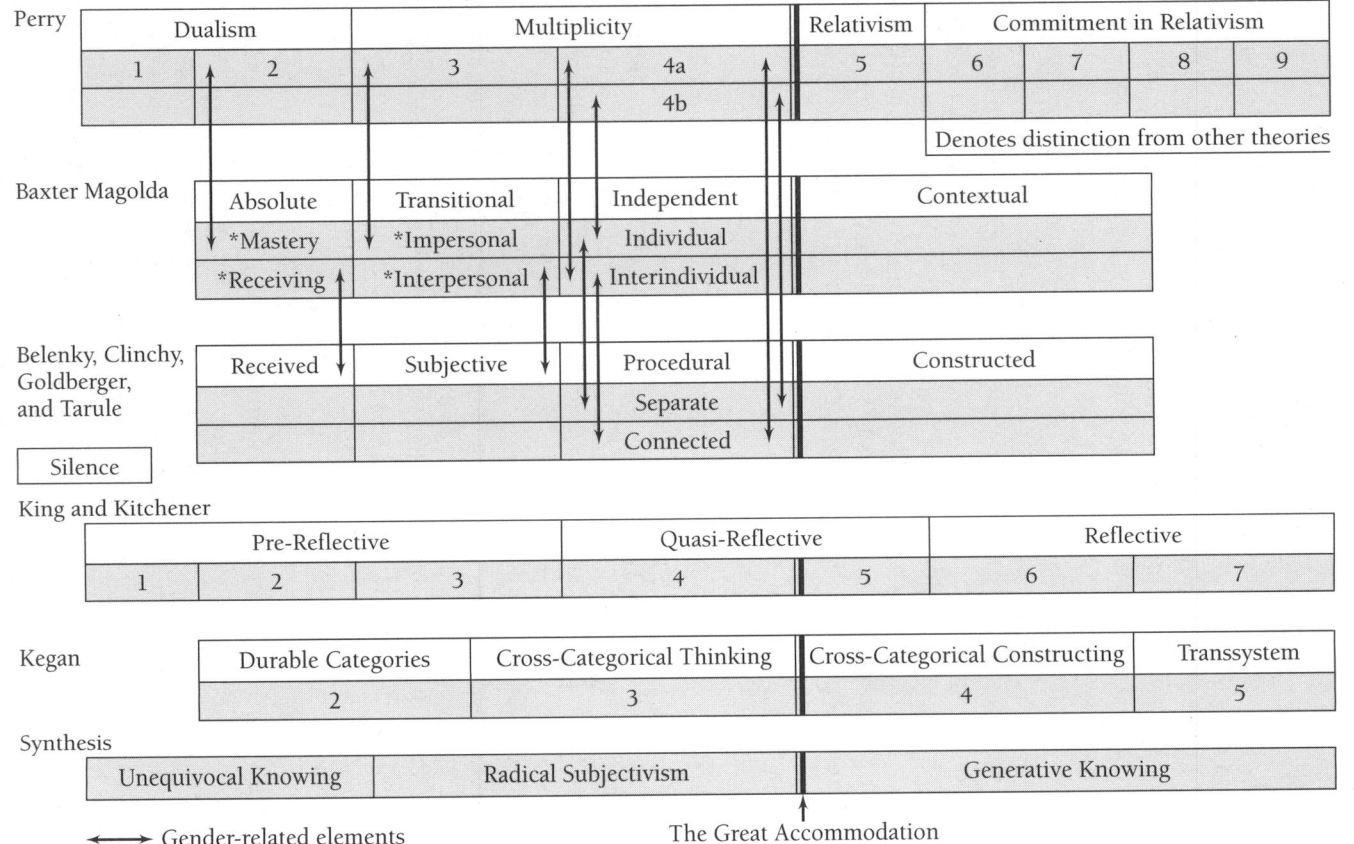

Perry

		Dualism			Multiplicity				Relativism	Commitment in Relativism			
1		2		3		4a			5	6	7	8	9
						4b							

Denotes distinction from other theories

Baxter Magolda

Absolute	Transitional	Independent	Contextual
*Mastery	*Impersonal	Individual	
*Receiving	*Interpersonal	Interindividual	

Belenky, Clinchy, Goldberger, and Tarule

Received	Subjective	Procedural	Constructed
		Separate	
		Connected	

Silence

King and Kitchener

	Pre-Reflective		Quasi-Reflective		Reflective	
1	2	3	4	5	6	7

Kegan

Durable Categories	Cross-Categorical Thinking	Cross-Categorical Constructing	Transsystem
2	3	4	5

Synthesis

Unequivocal Knowing	Radical Subjectivism	Generative Knowing

◄—► Gender-related elements   The Great Accommodation

Source: Based on a chart originally developed by Michael Poock.

focuses on *what* knowers are able to know rather than *how* they can know or justify knowledge claims. However, the *what* does not signify content but, rather, the level of complexity with which self, other, and relationships between the two can be known. Kegan's first order of consciousness is not included on the diagram, given its lack of applicability to college students.

Figure 7.1 also identifies gender-related patterns among the theories and highlights the point at which the "great accommodation" takes place in each theory, aligning the theories on this basis. Belenky, Clinchy, Goldberger, and Tarule's position of silence is indicated to be separate from their developmental scheme. We see it as both a predevelopmental phase in which an individual has not yet found a voice as a knower and as a state that may be experienced from any of the perspectives if forced on an individual externally (such as in the case of a student involved in a cult or an abusive relationship). An individual may have the experience of feeling silenced, which Belenky, Clinchy, Goldberger, and Tarule (1986, p. 146) refer to as a "problem with voice," to which even the most developed constructivist knowers are not "immune." Finally, Perry's last four positions are separated from the comparison because they diverge significantly from the other theories in that they focus on ethics and values rather than on meaning making or cognitive development.

The Role of Gender

The role that gender plays in the cognitive development of college students has been of interest to the higher education community for quite some time. The gender issues in the construction and methodology of the studies have already been addressed in the chapters devoted to each theory. However, an additional element for consideration is the suggestion by both Perry and Belenky, Clinchy, Goldberger, and Tarule that there are two paths over the continental divide of the "great accommodation" that appear to be gender related.

Perry describes this divergence in position 4. Perry and his colleagues found that the path students took appeared to be dictated by the balance between their tendency toward opposition on the one hand and adherence on the other, that is, by their relationship and identification with authority. Oppositional students did not identify with authority, which could be seen as the female-related pattern. By contrast, students tending toward adherence saw themselves as identifying with authority and could be considered male related. Perry describes the difference as authority-we-right (adherence) and authority-they-wrong, we-right (opposition). As discussed below, opposition could also entail authority-they-right, we-wrong, which describes a more strongly female-related pattern as experienced by the women in the study by Belenky, Clinchy, Goldberger, and Tarule (1986) and as described in Baxter Magolda's (1992) gender-related patterns.

Belenky, Clinchy, Goldberger, and Tarule describe an even more clearly gender-related pattern. The two paths were separate and connected knowing—

separate knowing being the male-related pattern and connected knowing the female-related pattern. Given the single-sex nature of the studies reported by Perry and by Belenky, Clinchy, Goldberger, and Tarule, we recognize that it is risky to label either of the patterns gender related. On the other hand, Baxter Magolda's population was a mix of men and women, and she did discover gender-related patterns in the cognitive development of her participants. She is very careful to emphasize that these are gender-*related* patterns, not gender-*dictated* patterns. These patterns relate to the differences found by Perry and Belenky, Clinchy, Goldberger, and Tarule. Baxter Magolda found evidence of the patterns throughout most of her developmental scheme, until they converged in contextual knowing. One of the issues that differentiated the two patterns was identification with authority: the male-related pattern tended to identify with authority; the female-related pattern did not. Another issue involved the role of relationships and peers. The female-related pattern focused on communion with others over agency, before melding together at contextual knowing; the male-related pattern focused on agency over communion, again before melding together.

Kegan (1994), like Rodgers (1990), argues that gender-related differences in ways of knowing are more a matter of style than structural difference. He recognizes nonnormative differences of epistemological *style* but rejects notions of hierarchical differences of epistemological *capacity*, or ability. Kegan further addresses the confusion of ideas of "separateness" or "independence" on the one hand with the fundamental construct of "autonomy" on the other. He asserts that "the self-authorizing capacity to 'decide for myself' does not also have to implicate the stylistic preference to 'decide by myself.' I can be self-authorizing in a relational way" (1994, p. 219). To prefer a relational, or connected, way of knowing does not reflect an inability to differentiate from any epistemological principle; rather, it indicates a "preferred way of relating to that from which one is differentiated" (Kegan, 1994, p. 219). Similar to Baxter Magolda's findings, Kegan's theory asserts that relational or separate constructions of experience are possible at each order of consciousness.

An obvious, but perhaps overlooked, point is Baxter Magolda's assertion that gender-related patterns of knowing disappear at advanced levels of cognitive development. Gilligan's work (1982) in the closely related field of moral development also suggests this convergence. It might be expected that if (or when) gender roles in society ameliorate or converge, the gender-related patterns of knowing also may merge earlier in the developmental scheme.

Culture and Cognitive Development

We look at the issue of culture and cognitive development in three ways. The first looks at subcultures in the United States that may have different patterns of cognitive development; the second looks at cultural transitions occurring in the dominant culture of the United States; and the third explores the potential influence of cultures outside the United States on future patterns of cognitive development in the United States.

The patterns described in the research cited in this volume are those discovered primarily among members of the dominant culture in American society. Yet in—or, more precisely, at the margins of—our society exist subcultures that differ from the dominant culture in ways that may influence the cognitive development of members of those cultures. Specifically, the collectivist cultures of Native American and Hispanic and Latino people may exert an influence where (according to the models built on dominant populations) gender-related patterns appear to fade. What we mean is that given the collectivist nature of these subcultures, the cognitive development of their members may be identified, for example, predominantly with the communion-focused female-related patterns described in Baxter Magolda's theory (1992). Unfortunately, there has been little cross-cultural research that examines issues of cognitive development (Hofer and Pintrich, 1997).

Another issue is what cognitive development of college students will look like twenty-five years from now. This question relates to the other two potential influences on cognitive developmental patterns. The first is the continuing movement of American society into what has been termed a postmodern age—a time when the roles of power, influence, values, and assumptions are highlighted, examined, and challenged. It can be expected that this shift will continue to shape the relationship between the individual and authority in our culture. It should, therefore, also have an influence on the cognitive developmental patterns of young people, especially insofar as how those patterns incorporate relationships with authority. Kegan (1994) argues that as a society, we are advancing and developing. He not only describes individual development but portrays the emergence of postmodern culture as a qualitatively advanced way in which society views knowledge and truth that calls for greater complexity and advanced ways of making meaning. In other words, the mental demands of modern life, which stem from the increasing complexity of living in today's world, are necessitating an evolution of consciousness or a new way of seeing ourselves in relation to the demands of our environment. Perhaps one reason why Perry and his colleagues could not more clearly describe positions beyond relativism was that, other than among countercultural individuals (such as rebels or revolutionaries) and transcultural individuals (such as inventors or philosophers), advanced stages of knowing were much less in evidence in the population they studied than they are today.

The other potential influence on future patterns of cognitive development relates to the globalization of culture and higher education. That is, as Western, positivistic culture, characterized by a mind-body split is influenced by Eastern, nonpositivistic, culture characterized by mind-body integration, perhaps we can expect to see an influence on the cognitive developmental patterns evidenced in American higher education. Currently, affective-based notions of knowing, such as intuition, are dismissed in our culture whereas in many Eastern cultures affective and cognitive approaches to knowing are more intertwined and mutually influential (Kegan, 1994). It could also be argued that in the process of cognitive development (especially as described by Baxter Magolda, 1992; Belenky, Clinchy, Goldberger, and Tarule, 1986; and Kegan, 1994) affect and emotion come to be more intimately incorporated in one's cognitive schemata as one develops advanced forms of meaning making. An implication of this idea could be that as we develop cognitively to the more advanced positions, we become more "Eastern" in outlook and sense making. Another distinction between positivistic and nonpositivistic cultures relates to how we come to know things. In positivism, in order to know an object, it must be separated from any context in order to discover the "truth" about it. In nonpositivistic cultures, objects cannot be known apart from their contexts. In a general way we might then say, at least according to some of the schemes of cognitive development reviewed in this volume, that Western (positivistic) culture is less cognitively advanced than Eastern (nonpositivistic) culture because contextual knowing is an advanced position of development.

Intentional Informal Assessment

All student affairs professionals practice assessment in their work with students. What kind of leader will this student be? How will this student do as an RA, orientation leader, or admissions tour guide? How does this student understand the consequences of her actions? How might she interpret a warning versus a referral to the discipline system? Will this student be able to understand and appreciate an alternative point of view? Why is this student having so much trouble with this particular professor or class?

These assessments are based most often and most strongly on our implicit theories, or theories-in-use (Argyris and Schön, 1974). These subconscious theories are derived from our experience, values, beliefs, and priorities, as well as from formal learning, such as completing a master's degree program, reading research literature, or attending professional development workshops. The theories-in-use are valuable to us because they serve as a knowledge and experience base to rely on in dealing with the problems and questions we face every day as professionals and to use in making assessments of the students and situations we face. Theories-in-use are also the major source of error in our actions because they include biases, stereotypes, and generalizations. They are subconscious and therefore difficult to clearly identify—and even more challenging to correct. It often takes overwhelming evidence to change one of our implicit theories. In many instances most evidence contradicting our informal theories is discarded as anomalous (Parker, 1977).

There are two ways through which we can assess the cognitive development of our students: formal assessment and informal assessment. Formal assessment typically involves the use of structured interviews or paper-and-pencil instruments that have been developed to assess students according to a particular theory, tested for reliability and validity, and published for use by trained professionals. We define informal assessment as estimating the level of cognitive development of an individual or group based on the evaluation of data collected through observation or dialogue. The focus of this section is on informal assessment primarily because that is how most professionals conduct assessment in their daily work with students. Indeed, rarely are the time, opportunity, or resources available to conduct formal assessments. However, we want to emphasize that we strongly support and encourage formal assessment when the situation warrants it and when resources are available. We refer those interested in identifying resources and techniques related to formal assessment of cognitive development to two excellent sources: King's chapter "Assessing Development from a Cognitive-Developmental Perspective" in *College Student Development: Theory and Practice for the 1990s* (1990) and Evans, Forney, and Guido-DiBrito's book *Student Development in College: Theory, Research, and Practice* (1998).

Although the main weakness of informal assessment has been identified as its potential for error (King, 1990), we believe it is imperative to focus on strengthening informal assessment. Our intent is to provide suggestions to help student affairs professionals improve their informal assessments of the developmental level of students on an individual and group basis. The relevance of knowing students' cognitive development level when interacting with them in an advising, disciplinary, or teaching capacity must be recognized. Without the ability to assess students' level of development, student affairs professionals will have only marginal success in understanding the students' perspective and encouraging their cognitive development. King (1990, p. 85) describes informal assessment as "generating hunches about students' developmental levels." *Intentional* informal assessment represents a middle ground between King's notion of informal assessment and formal assessment procedures. We assert that informal assessment can be more effective if done in a more conscious and intentional manner, thus reducing the error associated with traditional informal assessment. The intentional informal assessment techniques focus on determining the degree, strength, and pervasiveness of students' meaning making according to the three general levels of cognitive development identified earlier in this chapter: unequivocal, radical subjectivist, and generative.

When first developing and practicing the skill of intentional informal assessment, it is necessary to do so quite consciously. With practice, elements of formal theory will eventually be incorporated into one's theory-in-use. It is important to recognize that we do not discard theories-in-use and replace them with formal theories or with new informal theories. Instead, we develop our theories-in-use, make them more complex and sophisticated, and modify them. When we incorporate formal theory into our theories-in-use, the formal theory ceases to be an external, formal theory and instead becomes part of our internal, integrated knowledge base.

There are four elements to intentional informal assessment: knowledge and understanding of formal theory and data collection techniques; knowledge and understanding of self and one's theories-in-use; an appropriate mind-set related to the process of intentional informal assessment; and practice in and reflection on intentional informal assessment. These four elements do not represent a linear process. Instead, they are highly interactive and overlapping.

Knowledge and Understanding of Theory and Techniques. There are two basic knowledge bases in which student affairs professionals must be grounded: formal cognitive development theory and the techniques of qualitative data collection. We have assisted with the former by providing summaries of five major cognitive development theories and additional research on the social, cultural, and emotional influences on cognitive development. For a more in-depth understanding, we recommend that student affairs professionals read the original works. In this section we focus on the importance of possessing an understanding, as opposed to merely possessing knowledge, of formal theory and touch on the techniques of qualitative data collection. When one has *knowledge* of formal theory, one is separate from the theory and evaluates it from a position of distance and objectivity (Belenky, Clinchy, Goldberger, and Tarule, 1986). On the other hand, *understanding* formal theory implies personal acquaintance with, and recognition of a relationship to, the theory. Student affairs professionals need to go beyond knowledge of these theories and seek to understand them. Applying theory to one's own circumstances is typically the first step to understanding. In addition to a focus on one's own development, part of the process of understanding formal theory is cultivating the ability to recognize evidence of a student's developmental level in the context where the evidence occurs, such as in a staff meeting, class, disciplinary meeting, or advising session.

Skill in the qualitative data collection techniques of observation and clinical interviewing are also essential for student affairs professionals. In this area, too, one must go beyond mere knowledge of techniques and become trained and practiced in these abilities. It is important to recognize that observation implies more than just watching and clinical interviewing involves more than just conversation. Both are done with purpose and intent; there is a goal in the watching and conversing. Professionals must also watch and listen on two different levels: for the immediate content related to the issue at hand and for evidence of the cognitive developmental level. Good resources include campus workshops or classes focused on these techniques, as well as qualitative research textbooks (we especially recommend Strauss and Corbin, 1990; Spradley, 1979; and Patton, 1980).

Knowledge and Understanding of Self. This element of intentional informal assessment focuses on making conscious the subconscious in our professional work. The major source of error is one's own biases (King, 1990). We are typically blind to the filters through which we perceive and interpret our experience. We need greater self-knowledge in three areas: our own dominant patterns and positions in sense making; our biases, stereotypes, and assumptions related to the ways in which students (or types of students) make sense of the world; and our theories-in-use. This type of self-knowledge requires metacognition (the ability to think about and reflect on our thinking): How did I reach that conclusion? Was it the right one? How will I know whether it was right or wrong? In order to understand how students make sense of the world, we need to recognize how *we* make sense of the world. Where do we fall in Perry's positions, King and Kitchener's stages, or Kegan's model? Although our tendency might be to see ourselves as occupying the upper reaches of any of these theories, are there domains of knowledge or experience where we see the world more unequivocally or subjectively? This step will require knowledge of the formal theories and reflection on how we make sense of the world across multiple domains. We need to discover our biases, stereotypes, and assumptions related to subsets of students. What are our assumptions related to how subpopulations, such as sorority women, football players, honors students, African American students, Asian American students, or returning women students, make meaning? These assumptions can be positive ("Older students always have their act together.") or negative ("What did you expect? He's a football player."). Like our own level of sense making, biases, stereotypes, and assumptions provide subconscious filters through which we view the world that are difficult to recognize. Identifying assumptions requires reflection on our experience, openness to having our beliefs contradicted (an openness to evidence that is counter to our experience), and persistence (it takes time, given how strong and deeply ingrained most of our assumptions are).

A place to begin this process of discovery is to notice when something surprises you. Being surprised means something has happened that you did not expect. It also means you had an expectation—an assumption—that something else would happen. Reflect on what underlying assumption this surprise might represent and what evidence exists that it is an accurate or false assumption. All professionals are theory builders. We all draw on our experience and apply it to situations we face. How do I increase the motivation of my advisee? How do I deal with staff deficiencies? How do I get necessary resources from my supervisor? Argyris and Schön (1974) argue that in order to enhance our theories-in-use, we need to practice double-loop learning instead of single-loop learning. Single-loop learning results from the feedback we receive from the situation and incorporate into our practice for future use. For example, Peter is a freshman, and in my experience freshmen tend to view disciplinary situations fairly unequivocally. However, in a disciplinary interaction with Peter, I find that he actually views the world from a radical subjectivist perspective. I make a mental note of this, register Peter as an anomalous freshman, and recognize the importance of dealing with him on a more advanced level in our future interactions. This is single-loop learning: I have learned from my mistakes and have applied that learning to the situation at hand. Double-loop learning goes beyond single-loop learning in that, in addition to applying learning to the situation at hand, it applies the learning to the overall context, challenges the greater theory-in-use, and corrects mistakes. Is there a flaw in my theory that freshmen tend to view disciplinary situations unequivocally? Most professionals need consistent and overwhelming evidence to modify their theories-in-use. Argyris and Schön (1974) argue that intentional, reflective action can enhance our effectiveness and speed this process. Our goal becomes to constantly improve our theories-in-use rather than to defend them.

Appropriate Mind-Set. Several assumptions and attitudes will enhance one's ability to conduct intentional informal assessment when incorporated into one's theories-in-use:

Recognize that students are individuals who vary in the way they make sense of the world.

Recognize that students make sense of the world differently from the way you do.

Recognize that students' styles and levels of sense making differ depending on the context (such as classroom, residence hall, workplace) or the domain (such as religion, politics, academic subject) in which the interaction is taking place.

Recognize the need to hold one's hypotheses tentatively so that they can be modified by additional evidence, especially because mistakes in informal assessment are rarely self-correcting (Parker, 1977) and most often result in single-loop learning, not double-loop learning.

Practice and Reflection. The final element is truly the crux of intentional informal assessment. It requires putting the first three elements into practice in the context of professional activity, acting on one's findings, reflecting on the results, and applying that learning to the improvement of one's theories-in-use. It requires using data that emerge both from statements in context and from statements in response to intentionally crafted questions targeted at assessing cognitive level.

Application

Translating general and abstract theoretical constructs into specific and targeted developmental interventions is a task that requires concerted effort. As Perry (1970, p. 234) aptly observes: "Should our developmental scheme turn out to have the general validity which we believe it to have, the steps between its generalities and practical educational applications will remain many and arduous." The task also demands a degree of professional artistry of the type Schön (1987) believes necessary for reflective practitioners if they are to effectively use theory in complex and unique practical situations.

We assert that one of the most pivotal starting points in applying cognitive development theory is with Perry's conviction that "A fundamental belief in students is more important than anything else" (1970, p. 215). He goes on to say, "This fundamental belief is not a sentimental matter: it is a very demanding matter of realistically conceiving the student where he or she is and at the same time never losing sight of where he or she can be" (p. 215). Each of the theorists is explicit about the absolute obligation to confirm and recognize individuals in their current perspective, or way of making meaning, while at the same time acknowledging they are in the midst of a developmental process whereby they are continuously evolving cognitively. It is important to understand that none of the models make the assumption that an individual's reasoning fits only one stage at any point in time. Students typically have a range of developmental functioning, including an optimal level of which they are capable under supportive conditions and a functional level at which they operate the majority of the time (Fischer, 1980). In addition, Perry suggests that students can be in several different positions at once with respect to different subjects or experiences (Knefelkamp, 1999).

Transitions. College students might perhaps best be understood as beings in developmental transition, and this understanding is the reason that we specifically highlighted elements of transition in each of the theories. This fundamental concept of individuals being in motion is underscored particularly in the work of Perry and Kegan. Perry warns against imprisoning students in stages and urges educators to consider the notion that "perhaps development is all transition, and 'stages' are only resting points along the way" (1981, p. 78). Kegan (1982, pp. 7–8) asserts that the topic of his theory is the person, "where 'person' is understood to refer as much to an activity as to a thing—an ever progressive motion engaged in giving itself a new form." So, the notion of developmental transition becomes particularly important in understanding and applying cognitive development theory. Students can be seen as continually evolving in their forms of meaning making, involved in a journey in which they need and deserve "careful attention, recognition, confirmation, and company" along the way (Kegan, 1982, p. 126).

The Desirability of Development. One question that is important to address is whether development is desirable and whether educators should be involved in intentional attempts to stimulate the student's motion or evolution toward increasingly complex ways of making meaning. Perry is "adamantly against any notion of trying to force growth or development" (Knefelkamp, 1999, p. xiii) and considers the notion of force to be an anti-developmental concept. On the question of the "goodness" of development, Perry concludes that one position is not necessarily better than another.

However, several cognitive development theorists (such as Kegan, King, and Kitchener) suggest that some ways of making meaning are more well suited to the demands of a particular situation or more adaptive for various points in our lives. And, as Knefelkamp (1999, p. xxiv) reports, when asked if development was better, Perry was forced to concede, "it was a more adequate way of functioning in a complex world."

In illustrating this point, Kegan uses the analogy of driving a car. Most people of driving age can operate a car with an automatic transmission, and, in fact, most cars have this type of transmission. The only reason that an ability to drive a car with a manual transmission is valuable is if one is faced with the need to operate a car that does not have an automatic transmission. It is not that being able to use a manual transmission is inherently a better skill than being able to drive an automatic (though it is arguably a more complex skill). It is just that if you need to drive a car that requires this skill and you do not have it, you cannot deal effectively with the situation.

So, to the extent that we believe the demands of life and operating effectively in today's world require more complex cognitive skills than students typically have when entering college, educators have a responsibility to prepare college students to be competent in this world by aiding and supporting their evolution toward more adaptive and complex ways of making meaning. Although we must learn to use the theories of cognitive development to help us ascertain where individual students are in their own cognitive development process, we can anticipate that the majority of our effort will go to helping students prepare for and tentatively negotiate the "great accommodation" already described. This means abandoning unequivocal knowing and working through the uncomfortable temporary solution of radical subjectivism toward generative knowing—a way of meaning making that emphasizes students' role in the construction of knowledge and their self-authorship in terms of identity, emotions, and relationships. We have the chance to do this in our individual interactions with students in situations such as informal conversations, advising or counseling sessions, judicial hearings, or supervisions. We also have opportunities to be intentionally developmental in our interactions with student groups through advising, teaching, training, coaching, and programming. Some of these opportunities present themselves when we are helping a student or student group respond to a crisis that has arisen, forcing us into being developmental in a reactive manner. However, we also have and can create opportunities to take a proactive stance to aid student development in a more purposeful and intentional way.

Individual Interactions. Both Kegan (1994) and Baxter Magolda (1999) use the analogy of "being good company for the journey." Our individual interactions with students through daily contact and formal and informal conversation give us many opportunities to provide companionship in their journeys of cognitive development. Their current way of meaning making is, as Kegan (1994, p. 344) says, "worthy of our respect." In this vein, it is helpful to consider developmental theory a guide to asking better questions and an aid to understanding the individual rather than a framework into which we must force students by labeling them as "in" a certain stage.

However, Baxter Magolda (1992, pp. 348–349) reminds us that "dialogue continues the learning experience, whereas approval shuts it down." In order to be encouraging and enabling of their developmental process, we must not only confirm students as knowers and value their voices but also balance this confirmation with contradiction (Baxter Magolda, 1992). We must engage the students in dialogue that helps them process their experiences in a manner that leads to more complex ways of knowing. Baxter Magolda (1992) specifically suggests that we help students identify opportunities and make the most of them; discourage them from avoiding uncomfortable situations and transform these situations into educational opportunities; challenge their ideas while still affirming the value of their perspective; and compel them to take responsibility for their everyday lives.

Group Advising, Teaching, and Programming. Working with groups of students in an advisory, teaching, or programming role offers student affairs educators the chance to design environments that promote student development. Effective environments for student development combine confirmation, contradiction, and continuity (Kegan, 1982). Some students' choices, opinions, and approaches warrant confirmation; others warrant contradiction (along with confirmation that the students themselves are cared for and respected). Contradiction is inherent in students' participation in peer groups, student organizations, and other relational communities where genuine dialogue occurs and students encounter others with different experiences, values, and ways of knowing. Although too much contradiction can be threatening, contradiction that encourages exploration and reflection can remain in the productive range (Baxter Magolda, 1992). Student affairs educators can help students work through contradictions that occur naturally in interacting with others.

Continuity, or maintaining a connection with students, can offer a support system to students in developmental transition. However, we must expect to experience differences in our relationship with developing individuals as their perspectives on meaning making evolve. These "have much to do with the different person we ourselves have become in the organizing of the other" (Kegan, 1982, p. 133). For example, a valued adviser may go from being an all-knowing authority figure, to "just another opinion," to a valuable sounding board in the student's evolution of meaning making.

In working with student groups, there are several ways for student development educators to be intentionally developmental:

Designing the workshop, training, or program in such a way that it provides developmental challenges and supports

Choosing topics that will stimulate students to consider complex issues that require their active involvement in making meaning

Providing opportunities that require students to formulate a stance on an issue and explain their rationale

Constructing experiences that expose students to a variety of conflicting opinions, values, or ways of making meaning

Arranging activities that help students to reflect on their ways of knowing or to think about their thinking

Specific Developmental Interventions in Functional Areas. Much has been written from the perspectives of the various theories regarding specific developmental interventions in a variety of functional areas, such as financial aid advising (Coomes, 1992), career counseling (Knefelkamp and Slepitza, 1976), and working with residence halls (Stonewater, 1988). Space does not permit an in-depth exploration of these specific cognitive development interventions. However, Belenky, Clinchy, Goldberger, and Tarule (1986), Baxter Magolda (1992), and King and Kitchener (1994) have included specific chapters in their original texts addressing issues in the curriculum and cocurriculum.

Conclusion

As Baxter Magolda (1992, p. 362) reminds us, "offering students the opportunity for self-determination, for soaring and crashing, is essential if they are to function in complex ways when they leave college." The developmental process is not likely to be easy or comfortable. Perry (1978) emphasizes that there are costs to growth: leaving one way of making meaning is difficult, uncomfortable, and perhaps painful. He even speaks of a sense of loss the individual might experience that may involve a form of grieving for the comfort and ease of operating in the framework of making meaning that has just been left behind.

Finally, it is important to underscore the fact that cognitive development theory alone will not fully illuminate or adequately explain the developmental journeys of our students—their lives are complex, multifaceted, and full of possibilities. As Knefelkamp (1999, p. xiv) notes, Perry believed that "to understand what's going on, you need at least three theories." Cognitive development theory can be used with other models of student development, such as learning styles, psychosocial development, moral development, and identity development theories, to design environments and structure interactions that facilitate both cognitive growth and development in other areas. As students' thinking changes, so will their self-concepts, roles, and relationships.

REFERENCES

American College Personnel Association. *The Student Learning Imperative.* Washington, D.C.: American College Personnel Association, 1994.

American College Personnel Association and National Association of Student Personnel Administrators. *The Principles of Good Practice for Student Affairs.* Washington, D.C.: American College Personnel Association and National Association of Student Personnel Administrators, 1997.

Argyris, C., and Schön, D. *Theory in Practice: Increasing Professional Effectiveness.* San Francisco: Jossey-Bass, 1974.

Astin, A. *What Matters in College? Four Critical Years Revisited.* San Francisco: Jossey-Bass, 1993.

Bakan, D. *The Duality of Human Existence.* Boston: Beacon Press, 1966.

Barrow, J. C. *Fostering Cognitive Development.* San Francisco: Jossey-Bass, 1986.

Baxter Magolda, M. B. *Knowing and Reasoning in College: Gender-Related Patterns in Students' Intellectual Development.* San Francisco: Jossey-Bass, 1992.

Baxter Magolda, M. B. "The Integration of Relational and Impersonal Knowing in Young Adults' Epistemological Development." *Journal of College Student Development,* 1995, *36,* 205–216.

Baxter Magolda, M. B. "Journeys of the Mind, Voice, and Self: Charting a Path Through the Twenties." Address presented at the meeting of the American College Personnel Association, Atlanta, Georgia, March 1999.

Baxter Magolda, M. B. *Creating Contexts for Learning and Self-Authorship: Constructive-Developmental Pedagogy.* Nashville, Tenn.: Vanderbilt University Press, forthcoming.

Baxter Magolda, M. B., and Terenzini, P. T. "Learning and Teaching in the Twenty-First Century: Trends and Implications for Practice." In C. S. Johnson and H. E. Cheatham (eds.), *Higher Education Trends for the Next Century: A Research Agenda for Student Success.* Washington, D.C.: American College Personnel Association, 1999.

Bean, J. P., and Creswell, J. W. "Student Attrition Among Women at Liberal Arts Colleges." *Journal of College Student Personnel,* 1980, *21,* 320–327.

Belenky, M. F., Clinchy, B. M., Goldberger, N. R., and Tarule, J. M. *Women's Ways of Knowing: The Development of Self, Voice, and Mind.* New York: Basic Books, 1986.

Blake, L. "A Measure of Developmental Change: A Cross-Sectional Study." Paper presented at the annual meeting of the American Psychological Association, Washington, D.C., 1976.

Bless, H., Bohner, G., Schwarz, N., and Stack, F. "Mood and Persuasion: A Cognitive Response Analysis." *Personality and Social Psychology Bulletin,* 1990, *16,* 331–345.

Boekaerts, M. "Being Concerned with Well-Being and with Learning." *Educational Psychologist,* 1993, *28*(2), 149–167.

Brand, M. "Toward a Better Understanding of Undergraduate Music Education Majors: Perry's Perspective." *Bulletin of the Council for Research in Music Education,* 1988, *98,* 22–31.

Brophy, J. "Teacher-Student Interaction." In J. B. Dusk (ed.), *Teacher Expectancies.* Hillsdale, N.J.: Erlbaum, 1985.

Cabello, B., and Terrell, R. D. "Making Students Feel like Family: How Teachers Create Warm and Caring Classroom Climates." *Journal of Classroom Interaction,* 1994, *29*(1), 17–23.

Chickering, A. W., and Reisser, L. R. *Education and Identity.* (2nd ed.) San Francisco: Jossey-Bass, 1993.

Clinchy, B. M. "Connected and Separate Knowing: Toward a Marriage of Two Minds." In N. R. Goldberger, J. M. Tarule, B. M. Clinchy, and M. F. Belenky (eds.), *Knowledge,*

Difference, and Power: Essays Inspired by Women's Ways of Knowing. New York: Basic Books, 1996.

Connell, J. P. "Context, Self and Action: A Motivational Analysis of Self-System Processes Across the Lifespan." In D. Cicchetti (ed.), *The Self in Transition: Infancy to Childhood.* Chicago: University of Chicago Press, 1990.

Coomes, M. D. "Understanding Students: A Developmental Approach to Financial Aid Services." *Journal of Student Financial Aid,* 1992, 22(2), 23–31.

DeVries, R., and Kohlberg, L. *Constructivist Early Education: Overview and Comparison with Other Programs.* Washington, D.C.: National Association for the Education of Young Children, 1987.

Dewey, J. *How We Think: A Restatement of the Relation of Reflective Thinking to the Educative Process.* Lexington, Mass.: Heath, 1933.

Erikson, E. H. *Identity: Youth and Crisis.* New York: Norton, 1968.

Evans, N. J., Forney, D. S., and Guido-DiBrito, F. *Student Development in College: Theory, Research, and Practice.* San Francisco: Jossey-Bass, 1998.

Fischer, K. W. "A Theory of Cognitive Development: The Control and Construction of Hierarchies of Skills." *Psychological Review,* 1980, 87(6), 477–531.

Flores, B., Cousin, P. T., and Diaz, E. "Transforming Deficit Myths About Learning, Language and Culture." *Language Arts,* 1991, 68, 369–379.

Fowler, J. W. *Stages of Faith: The Psychology of Human Development and the Quest for Meaning.* San Francisco: HarperCollins, 1981.

Freire, P. *Pedagogy of the Oppressed.* New York: Continuum, 1970.

Gallagher, S. A. "The Road to Critical Thinking: The Perry Scheme and Meaningful Differentiation." *NASSP Bulletin,* 1998, 82, 12–20.

Gardner, H. *Multiple Intelligences: The Theory in Practice.* New York: Basic Books, 1993.

Gilligan, C. *In a Different Voice: Psychological Theory and Women's Development.* Cambridge, Mass.: Harvard University Press, 1982.

Giroux, H. *Theory and Resistance in Education: A Pedagogy for the Opposition.* New York: Bergin & Garvey, 1983.

Giroux, H. *Schooling and the Struggle for Public Life: Critical Pedagogy in the Modern Age.* Minneapolis: University of Minnesota Press, 1988.

Goldberger, N. "Ways of Knowing: Does Gender Matter?" In M. Roth Walsh (ed.), *Women, Men, and Gender: Ongoing Debates.* New Haven, Conn.: Yale University Press, 1997.

Goleman, D. *Emotional Intelligence.* New York: Bantam Books, 1995.

Good, T. "Two Decades of Research on Teacher Expectations: Findings and Future Directions." *Journal of Teacher Education* 1987, 38(6), 9–15.

Goodlad, J. *A Place Called School: Prospects for the Future.* New York: McGraw-Hill, 1984.

Harnett, R. T. "Involvement in Extracurricular Activities as a Factor in Academic Performance." *Journal of College Student Personnel,* 1965, 6, 272–274.

Hastorf, A. H., and Isen, A. M. *Cognitive Social Psychology.* New York: Elsevier, 1982.

Hersch, P. *A Tribe Apart: A Journey into the Heart of American Adolescence.* New York: Fawcett, 1998.

Hofer, B. K., and Pintrich, P. R. "The Development of Epistemological Theories: Beliefs About Knowledge and Knowing and Their Relation to Learning." *Review of Educational Research,* 1997, 67(1), 88–140.

Holland, J. L. *Making Vocational Choices: A Theory of Vocational Personalities and Work Environments.* Englewood Cliffs, N.J.: Prentice Hall, 1985.

Kagan, D. M. "How Schools Alienate Students at Risk: A Model for Examining Proximal Classroom Variables." *Educational Psychologist,* 1990, 25, 105–125.

Kegan, R. *The Evolving Self: Problem and Process in Human Development.* Cambridge, Mass.: Harvard University Press, 1982.

Kegan, R. *In Over Our Heads: The Mental Demands of Modern Life.* Cambridge, Mass.: Harvard University Press, 1994.

King, P. M. "William Perry's Theory of Intellectual and Ethical Development." In L. Kneflekamp, C. Widick, and C.A. Parker (eds.), *Applying New Developmental Findings.* New Directions for Student Services, no. 4. San Francisco: Jossey-Bass, 1978.

King, P. M. "Assessing Development from a Cognitive-Developmental Perspective." In D. G. Creamer (ed.), *College Student Development: Theory and Practice for the 1990s.* Lanham, Mass.: University Press of America, 1990.

King, P. M., and Baxter Magolda, M. B. "A Developmental Perspective on Learning." *Journal of College Student Development,* 1996, *37,* 163–173.

King, P. M., and Kitchener, K. S. *Developing Reflective Judgment: Understanding and Promoting Intellectual Growth and Critical Thinking in Adolescents and Adults.* San Francisco: Jossey-Bass, 1994.

Kitchener, K. S., and King, P. M. "Reflective Judgment: Concepts of Justification and Their Relationship to Age and Education." *Journal of Applied Developmental Psychology,* 1981, *2,* 89–116.

Kitchener, K. S., Lynch, C. L., Fischer, K. W., and Wood, P. K. "Developmental Range of Reflective Judgment: The Effect of Contextual Support and Practice on Developmental Stage." *Developmental Psychology,* 1993, *29*(5) 893–906.

Kloss, R. L. "A Nudge Is Best: Helping Students Through the Perry Scheme of Intellectual Development." *College Teaching,* 1994, *42*(4), 151–158.

Knefelkamp, L. L. "Introduction." In Perry, W. G., Jr., *Intellectual and Ethical Development in the College Years: A Scheme.* San Francisco: Jossey-Bass, 1999.

Knefelkamp, L. L., and Slepitza, R. "A Cognitive-Developmental Model of Career Development: An Adaptation of the Perry Scheme." *Counseling Psychologist,* 1976, *6*(3), 53–58.

Knefelkamp, L., Widick, C., and Parker, C. A. (eds.). *Applying New Developmental Findings.* New Directions for Student Services, no. 4. San Francisco: Jossey-Bass, 1978.

Kohlberg, L. "Stages and Sequence: The Cognitive-Developmental Approach to Socialization." In D. A. Goslin (ed.), *Handbook of Socialization Theory and Research.* Skokie, Ill.: Rand McNally, 1969.

Kroll, B. M. *Teaching Hearts and Minds: College Students Reflect on the Vietnam War in Literature.* Carbondale: Southern Illinois University Press, 1992.

Kuh, G. D. "The Other Curriculum: Out-of-Class Experiences Associated with Student Learning and Personal Development." *Journal of Higher Education,* 1995, *66,* 123–155.

Kuh, G. D., Schuh, J., and Whitt, E. J. *Involving Colleges: Successful Approaches to Fostering Student Learning and Development Outside the Classroom.* San Francisco: Jossey-Bass, 1991.

Kuhn, D. *The Skills of Argument.* Cambridge, England: Cambridge University Press, 1991.

Kurfiss, J. "Late Adolescent Development: A Structural Epistemological Perspective." Unpublished doctoral dissertation, University of Washington, 1975.

Kurfiss, J. "Sequentiality and Structure in a Cognitive Model of College Student Development." *Developmental Psychology,* 1977, *13,* 565–571.

Lahey, L., Souvaine, E., Kegan, R., Goodman, R., and Felix, S. *A Guide to the Subject-Object Interview: Its Administration and Interpretation.* Cambridge, Mass.: Harvard University, The Subject-Object Workshop, 1988.

Levine, A., and Cureton, J. *When Hope and Fear Collide: A Portrait of Today's College Students.* San Francisco: Jossey-Bass, 1998.

Li, A.K.F. "Peer Relations and Social Skills Training: Implications for the Multicultural Classroom." *Journal of Educational Issues of Language Minority Students,* 1992, *10,* 67–78.

Liddell, D. L. "Review of *Developing Reflective Judgment: Understanding and Promoting Intellectual Growth and Critical Thinking in Adolescents and Adults* by King and Kitchener." *Journal of College Student Development,* 1995, *36*(1), 94–96.

Love, P. G., and Goodsell Love, A. *Enhancing Student Learning: Intellectual, Social, and Emotional Integration.* ASHE-ERIC Higher Education Report no. 4. Washington, D.C.:

George Washington University, Graduate School of Education and Human Development, 1995.

Lundeberg, M. A., and Diemert Moch, S. "Influence of Social Interaction on Cognition: Connected Learning in Science." *Journal of Higher Education,* 1995, *66,* 312–335.

Martin, J. R. *Reclaiming a Conversation: The Ideal of the Educated Woman.* New Haven, Conn.: Yale University Press, 1985.

Maslow, A. H. *Motivation and Personality.* (3rd ed.) New York: HarperCollins, 1987.

McLaren, P. *Life in Schools: An Introduction to Critical Pedagogy in the Foundations of Education.* New York: Longman, 1989.

Meyer, P. "Intellectual Development: Analysis of Religious Content." *The Counseling Psychologist,* 1977, *6*(4), 47–50.

Myers, I. *Introduction to Type.* Palo Alto, Calif.: Consulting Psychologists Press, 1980.

Page, R. M., and Page, T. S. *Fostering Emotional Well-Being in the Classroom.* Boston: Jones and Bartlett, 1993.

Palmer, P. J. *To Know as We Are Known: Education as a Spiritual Journey.* San Francisco: HarperCollins, 1983.

Palmer, P. J. "Community, Conflict, and Ways of Knowing: Ways to Deepen Our Educational Agenda." *Change,* 1987, *19*(5), 20–25.

Parker, C. "On Modeling Reality." *Journal of College Student Personnel,* 1977, *18,* 419–425.

Pascarella, E., and Terenzini, P. T. *How College Affects Students.* San Francisco: Jossey-Bass, 1991.

Patton, M. Q. *Qualitative Evaluation Methods.* Thousand Oaks, Calif.: Sage, 1980.

Perry, W. G., Jr. *Intellectual and Ethical Development in the College Years: A Scheme.* Austin, Tex.: Holt, Rinehart and Winston, 1970.

Perry, W. G., Jr. "Sharing in the Costs of Growth." In C. A. Parker (ed.), *Encouraging Development in College Students.* Minneapolis: University of Minnesota Press, 1978.

Perry, W. G., Jr. "Cognitive and Ethical Growth: The Making of Meaning." In A. W. Chickering (ed.), *The Modern American College.* San Francisco: Jossey-Bass, 1981.

Peterson, C., and Seligman, M.E.P. "Causal Explanations as a Risk Factor for Depression: Theory and Evidence." *Psychological Review,* 1984, *91,* 347–374.

Piaget, J. R. *Science of Education and the Psychology of the Child.* New York: Viking Penguin, 1969.

Piaget, J. R., and Inhelder, B. *Psychology of the Child.* New York: Basic Books, 1971.

Piper, T. D., and Rodgers, R. F. "Theory-Practice Congruence: Factors Influencing the Internalization of Theory." *Journal of College Student Development,* 1992, *33,* 117–123.

Rodgers, R. F. "Recent Theories and Research Underlying Student Development." In D. G. Creamer (ed.), *College Student Development: Theory and Practice for the 1990s.* Lanham, Md.: University Press of America, 1990.

Rogoff, B. *Apprenticeship in Thinking: Cognitive Development in a Social Context.* New York: Oxford University Press, 1990.

Rubin, R. A., and Henzl, S. A. "Cognitive Complexity, Communication Competence, and Verbal Ability." *Communication Quarterly,* 1984, *32*(4), 263–270.

Ruddick, S. "Maternal Thinking." *Feminist Studies,* 1980, *6,* 70–96.

Sanford, N. *The American College: A Psychological and Social Interpretation of the Higher Learning.* New York: Wiley, 1962.

Schön, D. A. *Educating the Reflective Practitioner.* San Francisco: Jossey-Bass, 1987.

Schroeder, C. C. "The Student Learning Imperative: Implications for Student Affairs." *The Journal of College Student Development,* 1996, *37*(2), 118–122.

Seiler, W. J. *Communication in the Contemporary Classroom.* Austin, Tex.: Holt, Rinehart and Winston, 1989.

Shor, I. *Empowering Education: Critical Teaching for Social Change.* Chicago: University of Chicago Press, 1992.

Spradley, J. *The Ethnographic Interview.* Austin, Tex.: Holt, Rinehart and Winston, 1979.

Springer, L., Terenzini, P. T., Pascarella, E. T., and Nora, A. "Influences on College Students' Orientations Toward Learning for Self-Understanding." *Journal of College Student Development,* 1995, *36*(1), 5–18.

Stonewater, B. B. "Informal Developmental Assessment in the Residence Halls: A Theory to Practice Model." *NASPA Journal,* 1988, *25*(4), 267–273.

Strauss, A., and Corbin, J. *Basics of Qualitative Research: Grounded Theory Procedures and Techniques.* Thousand Oaks, Calif.: Sage, 1990.

Sylvester, R. "How Emotions Affect Learning." *Educational Leadership,* 1994, *52,* 60–65.

Tarule, J. M. "A Letter to Paulo Freire." In P. Freire (ed.), *Mentoring the Mentor: A Critical Dialogue with Paulo Freire.* New York: Lang, 1997.

Thayer, R. E. *The Biopsychology of Mood and Arousal.* New York: Oxford University Press, 1989.

Thoma, G. A. "The Perry Framework and Tactics for Teaching Critical Thinking in Economics." *Journal of Economic Education,* 1993, *24*(2), 128–135.

Tinto, V., and Goodsell, A. "Freshman Interest Groups and the First-Year Experience: Constructing Student Communities in a Large University." *Journal of the Freshman Year Experience,* 1993, *6*(1), 7–28.

Tinto, V., Russo, P., and Kadel, S. "Constructing Educational Communities: Increasing Retention in Challenging Circumstances." *American Association of Community Colleges Journal,* 1994, *64,* 26–29.

Vygotsky, L. S. *Mind in Society.* Cambridge, Mass.: Harvard University Press, 1978.

Weinstein, R. "Perceptions of Classroom Processes and Student Motivation: Children's Views of Self-Fulfilling Prophecies." In C. Ames and R. Ames (eds.), *Research on Motivation in Education.* Vol. 3: *Goals and Cognition.* Orlando, Fla.: Academic Press, 1989.

Welte, S. L. "Transforming Educational Practice: Addressing Underlying Epistemological Assumptions." *Review of Higher Education,* 1997, *20* (2), 199–213.

Wingspread Group on Higher Education. *An American Imperative: Higher Expectations for Higher Education.* Racine, Wisc.: Johnson Foundation, 1993.

INDEX

ness (second), 68, 69

Eastern cultural influences, 58, 84–85
Education: as alienating to connected knowers, 25; as alienating to received knowers, 20–21; "banking method" of, 57; importance of emotion in, 60–61
Ellis, A., 61
Emotional influences on cognitive development, 59–62; and college outcomes, 61–62; positive and negative, 62, 63; research on, 60–62
Environments for student development: effective, 92; holding, 75–76
Epistemological reflection model, 3, 29–40; application to student affairs, 37–39; conclusion, 39; longitudinal study description, 30, 80; patterns of knowing, 30–37; six principles underlying the, 29–30; Welte's analysis of, 37
Epistemological style versus capacity, 83
Erikson, E., 65
Ethical and moral development, and Perry's nine positions, 8
Ethnicity. See Diversity of college students
Evans, N. J., 5, 86
Events, transformative and transitional, 19, 71
Evidence: ability to compare and contrast, 47; anomalous, 85
The Evolving Self (Kegan), 65–66
Experience, knowledge from personal, 24–25

Fear, and creative conflict, 63
Feelings: and intellect, 60–61; and thinking, 53
Fischer, K. W., 42, 90
Formal assessment. See Assessment
Forney, D. S., 5, 86
Freire, P., 57
Friends, relationships with, 33, 55–56, 75–76
Functional level of reasoning, 49, 90

Gardner, H., 1
Gender of participants in studies, 6, 14, 17, 30, 41, 58
Gender-related elements: absolute know-

ing receiving or mastery, 32–33; composite view of, 80, 81; in friendships, 55; interindividual and individual, 35, 36, 38; interpersonal and impersonal, 33–34; merging or convergence of, 36, 79, 83; not gender-dictated, 83; theories on divergence of, 82–83
Generative knowing, 78, 79–80, 91
Gilligan, C., 17
Globalization of culture, 84–85
Goldberger, N. R., 3, 14, 17–27, 32, 53–54, 55, 56, 58, 78, 79, 81, 82–83
Goleman, D., 59, 60, 61–62
Goodlad, J., 59
Goodsell, A., 62
Grades, emotions as predictors of, 62
Grading systems, questioning, 9–10
Graduate students, 80
Graduation, developmental status upon, 14
The great accommodation, 79, 80; helping students with, 91; theories chart aligned by, 81
Group advising, teaching, and programming, 92–93
Groups. See Student groups
Growing pains, cognitive development, 93
Guido-DiBrito, F., 5, 86
Guthrie, V. L., 3

Harvard and Radcliffe students, 6
Hastorf, A. H., 60
Hearing oneself think, 23
Henzl, S. A., 54
Hersch, P. A., 58, 59
Hidden multiplists, 22
Hofer, B. K., 41, 59, 84
Holding environments, order of consciousness, 75–76

Identity, an enduring sense of, 72–73
Ideology, capacity of making an, 72
Ill-structured problems: definition of, 42; in student life and student affairs work, 50
Impersonal knowing pattern, 33–34, 38
Implications for student affairs professionals: of Baxter Magolda's model, 37–39; of cultural influences on students, 59; of emotional influences on students, 62–63; intentional informal assessment and, 85–89; of interper-

Back Issue/Subscription Order Form

Copy or detach and send to:
Jossey-Bass Inc., Publishers, 350 Sansome Street, San Francisco, CA 94104-1342

Call or fax toll free!
Phone 888-378-2537 6AM-5PM PST; Fax 800-605-2665

Back issues: Please send me the following issues at $23 each
(Important: please include series initials and issue number, such as SS90)

1. SS _____

_____

_____

$ _____ Total for single issues

$ _____ Shipping charges (for single issues **only;** subscriptions are exempt
from shipping charges): Up to $30, add $5^{50} • $30^{01}–$50, add $6^{50}
$50^{01}–$75, add $7^{50} • $75^{01}–$100, add $9 • $100^{01}–$150, add $10
Over $150, call for shipping charge

Subscriptions   Please ❑ start   ❑ renew my subscription to *New Directions
for Higher Education* for the year _____ at the following rate:

❑ Individual $58   ❑ Institutional $104
NOTE: Subscriptions are quarterly, and are for the calendar year only.
Subscriptions begin with the spring issue of the year indicated above.
For shipping outside the U.S., please add $25.

$ _____ Total single issues and subscriptions (CA, IN, NJ, NY, and DC
residents, add sales tax for single issues. NY and DC residents must
include shipping charges when calculating sales tax. NY and Canadian
residents only, add sales tax for subscriptions)

❑ Payment enclosed (U.S. check or money order only)

❑ VISA, MC, AmEx, Discover Card #_____ Exp. date_____

Signature _____ Day phone _____

❑ Bill me (U.S. institutional orders only. Purchase order required)

Purchase order #_____

Name _____

Address _____

_____

_____

Phone_____ E-mail _____

For more information about Jossey-Bass Publishers, visit our Web site at:
www.josseybass.com   **PRIORITY CODE = ND1**

United States Postal Service

Statement of Ownership, Management, and Circulation

1. Publication Title	2. Publication Number		3. Filing Date
NEW DIRECTIONS FOR STUDENT SERVICES	0 1 6 4 – 7 9 7 0		9/30/99

4. Issue Frequency	5. Number of Issues Published Annually	6. Annual Subscription Price
QUARTERLY	4	$ 58 – indiv. $104 – inst.

7. Complete Mailing Address of Known Office of Publication *(Not printer) (Street, city, county, state, and ZIP+4)*
350 SANSOME STREET
SAN FRANCISCO, CA 94104
(SAN FRANCISCO COUNTY)

Contact Person
ROGER HUNT
Telephone
(415) 782-3232

8. Complete Mailing Address of Headquarters or General Business Office of Publisher *(Not printer)*
JOSSEY-BASS INC., PUBLISHERS
(ABOVE ADDRESS)

9. Full Names and Complete Mailing Addresses of Publisher, Editor, and Managing Editor *(Do not leave blank)*

Publisher *(Name and complete mailing address)*
JOSSEY-BASS INC., PUBLISHERS
(ABOVE ADDRESS)

Editor *(Name and complete mailing address)*
JOHN H. SCHUH
N243 LAGOMARCINO HALL
IOWA STATE UNIVERSITY
AMES, IA 50011

Managing Editor *(Name and complete mailing address)*
NONE

10. Owner *(Do not leave blank. If the publication is owned by a corporation, give the name and address of the corporation immediately followed by the names and addresses of all stockholders owning or holding 1 percent or more of the total amount of stock. If not owned by a corporation, give the names and addresses of the individual owners. If owned by a partnership or other unincorporated firm, give its name and address as well as those of each individual owner. If the publication is published by a nonprofit organization, give its name and address.)*

Full Name	Complete Mailing Address
JOHN WILEY & SONS INC.	605 THIRD AVENUE
	NEW YORK, NY 10158-0012

11. Known Bondholders, Mortgagees, and Other Security Holders Owning or Holding 1 Percent or More of Total Amount of Bonds, Mortgages, or Other Securities. If none, check box ——▶ ☐ None

Full Name	Complete Mailing Address
SAME AS ABOVE	SAME AS ABOVE

12. Tax Status *(For completion by nonprofit organizations authorized to mail at nonprofit rates) (Check one)*
The purpose, function, and nonprofit status of this organization and the exempt status for federal income tax purposes:
☐ Has Not Changed During Preceding 12 Months
☐ Has Changed During Preceding 12 Months *(Publisher must submit explanation of change with this statement)*

PS Form **3526,** September 1998 *(See Instructions on Reverse)*

---

13. Publication Title	14. Issue Date for Circulation Data Below
NEW DIRECTIONS FOR STUDENT SERVICES	SUMMER 1999

15. Extent and Nature of Circulation		Average No. Copies Each Issue During Preceding 12 Months	No. Copies of Single Issue Published Nearest to Filing Date
a. Total Number of Copies *(Net press run)*		1888	1782
b. Paid and/or Requested Circulation	(1) Paid/Requested Outside-County Mail Subscriptions Stated on Form 3541. *(Include advertiser's proof and exchange copies)*	789	781
	(2) Paid In-County Subscriptions *(Include advertiser's proof and exchange copies)*	0	0
	(3) Sales Through Dealers and Carriers, Street Vendors, Counter Sales, and Other Non-USPS Paid Distribution	143	153
	(4) Other Classes Mailed Through the USPS	0	0
c. Total Paid and/or Requested Circulation *[Sum of 15b. (1), (2),(3),and (4)]* ▶		932	934
d. Free Distribution by Mail *(Samples, complimentary, and other free)*	(1) Outside-County as Stated on Form 3541		
	(2) In-County as Stated on Form 3541		
	(3) Other Classes Mailed Through the USPS	94	49
e. Free Distribution Outside the Mail *(Carriers or other means)*		70	70
f. Total Free Distribution *(Sum of 15d. and 15e.)* ▶		164	119
g. Total Distribution *(Sum of 15c. and 15f)* ▶		1096	1053
h. Copies not Distributed		792	729
i. Total *(Sum of 15g. and h.)* ▶		1888	1782
j. Percent Paid and/or Requested Circulation *(15c. divided by 15g. times 100)*		85%	89%

16. Publication of Statement of Ownership
☒ Publication required. Will be printed in the WINTER 1999 issue of this publication.   ☐ Publication not required.

17. Signature and Title of Editor, Publisher, Business Manager, or Owner
Susan E. Lewis   SUSAN E. LEWIS   DIRECTOR OF PERIODICALS   Date 9/30/99

I certify that all information furnished on this form is true and complete. I understand that anyone who furnishes false or misleading information on this form or who omits material or information requested on the form may be subject to criminal sanctions (including fines and imprisonment) and/or civil sanctions (including civil penalties).

Instructions to Publishers

1. Complete and file one copy of this form with your postmaster annually on or before October 1. Keep a copy of the completed form for your records.

2. In cases where the stockholder or security holder is a trustee, include in items 10 and 11 the name of the person or corporation for whom the trustee is acting. Also include the names and addresses of individuals who are stockholders who own or hold 1 percent or more of the total amount of bonds, mortgages, or other securities of the publishing corporation. In item 11, if none, check the box. Use blank sheets if more space is required.

3. Be sure to furnish all circulation information called for in item 15. Free circulation must be shown in items 15d, e, and f.

4. Item 15h., Copies not Distributed, must include (1) newsstand copies originally stated on Form 3541, and returned to the publisher, (2) estimated returns from news agents, and (3), copies for office use, leftovers, spoiled, and all other copies not distributed.

5. If the publication had Periodicals authorization as a general or requester publication, this Statement of Ownership, Management, and Circulation must be published; it must be printed in any issue in October or, if the publication is not published during October, the first issue printed after October.

6. In item 16, indicate the date of the issue in which this Statement of Ownership will be published.

7. Item 17 must be signed.

Failure to file or publish a statement of ownership may lead to suspension of Periodicals authorization.

PS Form **3526,** September 1998 *(Reverse)*